Praise for  *You Die*

"The first time I heard the story that drives the content of this book, tears streamed down my face. My good friend Randy Frazee and I share a mutual passion for what comes next after this life that flows from our deep loss, and I'm so thankful he's sharing the profound truths about real hope that he's learned on his journey with us through this powerful book."

—Steven Curtis Chapman, Grammy
Award–winning singer and songwriter

"We've all wrestled with the concept of what it is going to be like after we die and beyond. Although we'll never fully grasp the wonders until we get there, Randy paints a beautiful picture from the scriptures. I've known Randy for a while now and his heart truly is one to bring encouragement to the body of believers. So be encouraged!"

—Jeremy Camp, five-time Dove Award–
winning singer and songwriter

"This is a learned, lambent, superbly crafted, grippingly absorbing treatment of the end times. A belter of a book that calls across the generations. Save an evening to read it, and you'll savor it for a lifetime."

—Dr. Leonard Sweet, professor and
bestselling author, Absecon, New Jersey

"This book is a super-practical, biblical guide that I would feel comfortable giving to anyone I know—believer or non. It's chock-full of scripture, and I can't wait to use it as a tool to teach my children about the deep truths of heaven. Randy is truly a man of God, and I'm grateful to call him a friend!"

—Francesca Battistelli, Grammy
Award–winning artist

"Usually prior to endorsing a book, I skim through it. That was impossible with *What Happens After You Die.* You'll want to devour every word and scripture in this book. Prepare to be taught, encouraged, and challenged from God's Word and Randy's heart."

—Dave Stone, senior pastor, Southeast
Christian Church, Louisville, Kentucky

"The idea that all we will do is cast our crowns and cry 'Holy, Holy, Holy' for the rest of eternity causes a sense of dread and boredom for most men I know. This is all we'll do in heaven? Randy Frazee gives so much more insight into the adventure God has in store for us for all eternity!"

—Todd Smith, lead singer of Selah, the multi-
platinum and Dove Award–winning group

"We all have questions when it comes to life's most confusing and danger-ous transition. His answers are wonderfully refreshing, honest, and pow-erfully biblical."

—Kenton Beshore, senior pastor,
Mariners Church, California

WHAT *Happens* AFTER YOU DIE

A BIBLICAL GUIDE
TO PARADISE,
HELL, *and* LIFE AFTER DEATH

RANDY FRAZEE

NELSON
BOOKS
An Imprint of Thomas Nelson

© 2017 by Randy Frazee

Published in Nashville, Tennessee, by Nelson Books, an imprint of Thomas Nelson. Nelson Books and Thomas Nelson are registered trademarks of HarperCollins Christian Publishing, Inc.

Thomas Nelson titles may be purchased in bulk for educational, business, fund-raising, or sales promotional use. For information, please e-mail SpecialMarkets@ThomasNelson.com.

Any Internet addresses, phone numbers, or company or product information printed in this book are offered as a resource and are not intended in any way to be or to imply an endorsement by Thomas Nelson, nor does Thomas Nelson vouch for the existence, content, or services of these sites, phone numbers, companies, or products beyond the life of this book.

Unless otherwise indicated, Scripture quotations are taken from the Holy Bible, New International Version', NIV* Copyright ©1973, 1978, 1984, 2011 by Biblica, Inc.* Used by permission. All rights reserved worldwide.

Scripture quotatons marked ESV are taken from the ESV* Bible (The Holy Bible, English Standard Version'). Copyright © 2001 by Crossway, a publishing ministry of Good News Publishers. Used by permission. All rights reserved.

Scripture quotations marked KJV are taken from the Holy Bible, King James Version (public domain).

Quotations marked NRSVA are taken from the New Revised Standard Version Bible: Anglicised Edition, copyright © 1989, 1995 the Division of Christian Education of the National Council of the Churches of Christ in the United States of America. Used by permission. All rights reserved.

ISBN 978-0-718086039 (eBook)

Library of Congress Cataloging-in-Publication Data

Names: Frazee, Randy, author.
Title: What happens after you die : a biblical guide to paradise, hell, and
  life after death / Randy Frazee.
Description: Nashville : Thomas Nelson, 2017.
Identifiers: LCCN 2016036315 | ISBN 9780718086046
Subjects: LCSH: Future life--Biblical teaching. | Future life--Christianity.
Classification: LCC BS2545.F88 F73 2017 | DDC 236/.2--dc23 LC record available at
  https://lccn.loc.gov/2016036315

17 18 19 20 21 LSC 10 9 8 7 6 5 4 3 2 1

To Don, Teresa, and Jo Ann,
my awesome big brother and two beautiful sisters

Other Books by Randy Frazee

The Heart of the Story

Think, Act, Be Like Jesus

Believe (General Editor)

The Christian Life Profile Assessment

The Connecting Church 2.0

Believe 365 Day Devotional (coauthored with Rozanne Frazee)

Real Simplicity (coauthored with Rozanne Frazee)

Renovation of the Heart, Student Edition

(coauthored with Dallas Willard)

Contents

Introduction

What's Next?

IT WAS DECEMBER 1999. THE WORLD WAS WORRIED about Y2K, the predicted worldwide crashing of the Internet. I, on the other hand, was firmly stuck in the twentieth century, worried about my mother in Cleveland, Ohio. For several months, she had complained she wasn't feeling well. Each time we talked, the circumstances worsened. My family—living in Fort Worth, Texas, at the time—had already booked flights to spend the Christmas holiday in Cleveland with our extended families, but because of my mom's condition, I decided to go up three days earlier to be with my mom and see if I could help her to feel better.

The doctors had already tested my mom for colon and liver cancer; the tests had come back negative, so they were unable to pinpoint the problem. Pulling every string I knew, I was able to arrange an appointment for my mom on supershort notice at the renowned Cleveland Clinic. When I arrived at our cottage in Mentor-on-the-Lake and walked into the living room, my mother was lying on the couch. I tried not to be startled at how gaunt and sickly she looked, but of course she noticed. It was nearly impossible to hide anything from Mom. I assured her that I had arrived to help her get healthy again, and we all went to bed that night.

My dad slept in their bedroom, while my mother and younger sister slept in the living room. I slept in a room right off the living room. For many hours during that night, I lay awake, listening to the painful moans and sounds of vomiting coming from my mother. It was truly unbearable to hear these cries and be able to do nothing about it. Tomorrow, I thought, would be different.

My hopes rose with the first ray of sunshine that peered through my bedroom window. We needed to travel about an hour to the hospital, and we planned to take my parents' Econoline travel van, which they had originally purchased to see the country. When it came time to leave, my mother said she was in too much pain to walk to the van, so I put my mom on my back, just as she had done for me so many times when I was a little kid, and carried her to the van. With every step I took, my mother literally screamed in pain. At that moment, a layer of innocence was peeled back in my life.

My dad drove the van while my mom lay on the back bench. I sat on the edge of the bench to talk with and tend to my mother. About ten minutes into the trip, my mom took me on another road trip down memory lane.

The year was 1977. Having arrived at home from high school in the afternoon, I plopped myself down on the couch to catch an episode of the soap opera *One Life to Live*. (Before criticism leaks from the lips of you millennials, keep in mind there was no Internet and very few television stations back then, so the programming was quite limited.) My mom walked in. She told me she had been to visit the youth pastor of the church I attended. My folks didn't go to church, but I had started attending a Baptist church three years earlier.

My parents were having marital trouble, and my mom had gone to get some counseling. My pastor didn't fix her marriage, but he did tell my mom about Jesus. My mom shared how he had led her through the Sinner's Prayer. I knew exactly the prayer she was referring to. He had led me through that same prayer three years earlier as I knelt by a folding chair with him in the church's youth room.

Now, sitting in the van on my way to the hospital, my mom asked me if I remembered that day. "Oh, yes, Mom. It meant the world to me," I answered.

Then she asked me a question I didn't see coming.

"Son," she said, "is it enough?" In other words, was that prayer of faith, prayed long ago, enough to ensure that she would be with God when she died?

I immediately responded, as confidently as I could, "Why, yes, Mom, it is enough."

She was putting her spiritual house in order. I, on the other hand, was not ready for that conversation.

When we arrived at the hospital, I went in and informed the staff that my mom needed a gurney to get to the floor and suite she had been assigned. Once my mom had been admitted, I sat in the waiting room with a mild confidence that these renowned doctors would be able to put my mother back together again.

It couldn't have been thirty minutes before the oncologist asked to talk with me. She, in a very tender voice, informed me that my mom had advanced pancreatic cancer, and they were going to move her to palliative care. I had never heard the word *palliative* before. Turned out the palliative care unit was a place where they eased the pain without curing the disease. The choleric side of my temperament showed up.

"I don't understand. I came here for you famous doctors to heal my mother."

With a gentle response I didn't deserve, the doctor replied, "I know it's hard. I lost my mom to colon cancer. It's time for you to shift gears from helping your mom heal to helping her die."

A tsunami of grief rushed over my soul.

The doctor said we had perhaps as much as a week, or maybe only a few days. After I called my wife, my sister living in Minnesota, and my brother living in Pennsylvania, I headed to the chapel to have a talk with God.

Gratefully the room was empty. Without much thought I did exactly what David had done when the prophet Nathan had told him that his infant son was going to die: I lay prostrate on the floor and began to wail and plead with God (2 Samuel 12:15–17). My mom was only sixty-two. This was not an event I had anticipated visiting me so soon. I had been a Christian for twenty-five years, but I could sense that the very fabric of my faith was starting to unravel.

My first instinct was to pray for a miraculous healing. I shamelessly bargained with God, much as Abraham had done when he was trying to change God's mind about destroying Sodom and Gomorrah. "God, would you save my mom if I promise to . . . ?" Once that request was firmly submitted, I turned my attention to my mom's earlier question. "God, I told my mom that a simple prayer of faith to receive Christ was enough, but if something more is required, then I need to know now while there is still time."

There had always been those passages in the Bible, even in the teachings of Jesus, that gave me pause on the *sola fide*, or "faith alone," message. I was ready in that moment for God to reveal the absolute truth to me so I could get it to my mom before it was too late.

Three days later, my mom died.

At first there was relief that my mom was no longer in pain and suffering. Pancreatic cancer literally sucks the life out of a person with every breath. My mom knew she was going to die, and she was afraid. I saw it on her face. She wanted to be strong, but she was frightened. To date this is one of the hardest things I have ever watched. As a result, something switched inside of me, where the very core of my belief system resided.

The more I thought about it, the more I struggled to believe that at the moment my mother breathed her last breath, her spirit exited her body and went to be anywhere, let alone with the Lord. I just didn't have a mental model for this concept, and yet we Christians base our entire hope on this reality. I knew some say they have, but I had never personally met a spirit being. Did such beings really exist?

My mind continued to wander without permission. Even if life after death was true, and a person's spirit did exit the body, the idea of a naked spirit entering into the heavens, floating on clouds forever, and continually singing worship songs—maybe with earned wings, like Clarence in *It's a Wonderful Life*—just didn't seem all that compelling to me. It was certainly better than the scriptural alternative, but it was still not something I craved.

"I don't believe in heaven," I whispered.

I can't believe I said it out loud, but I did. While I feared lightning might strike, I also felt liberated. It was in that moment, when I confessed that I didn't really believe what I had always been taught about heaven, that I felt freed up to seek truth. Since then I have discovered that until we genuinely confess our unbelief, we will never pursue something worth believing.

UNTIL WE GENUINELY CONFESS OUR UNBELIEF, WE WILL NEVER PURSUE SOMETHING WORTH BELIEVING.

At the turn of the century, the Internet didn't end up crashing, but I did. So I went on a journey to discover the truth about the afterlife. With no denominational ax to grind or sermon to prepare, I started to crack open the Bible to find what was really there. Even if what I found was not comforting or what I had hoped, at least it would be true. Jesus said, "You will know the truth, and the truth will set you free" (John 8:32). I did believe that.

It didn't take long to discover I was not alone. Many rich-thinking theologians have been proclaiming the need for clarity on the afterlife for years in their textbooks and lectures. Theology professor and author Dr. Roger Olson offered these poignant words:

> Christian theologians and leaders of all Christian traditions ought to focus attention on helping untutored lay Christians grasp essential Christian belief about life beyond death and separate that from the welter of folk beliefs that they tend to pick up from movies, television programs, popular literature and songs. Christian ministers of all denominations need to proclaim the

blessed hope of future resurrection at funerals and strictly avoid pandering to what relatives of the deceased want to hear.[1]

What I found and now believe 100 percent in my head and 85 percent in my heart (I am still a work in progress) makes up the content of this book. It is a no-frills, no-nonsense approach. It is a simple "ask the question and answer it only from what the Scriptures tell us" approach. That is what I am shooting for here.

Here are the five questions I will seek to answer:

- *Is Jesus enough?*

  This is the question my mom asked in the back of the van just before her death. What a great question, Mom. She had taken Jesus up on an offer he made. Was receiving this offer really enough? Really? In this chapter we will line up scriptures side by side that answer this question explicitly and not be afraid to let the scriptures speak for themselves as we search for the gospel truth.

- *What happens to me if I die without Christ?*

  What is the fate of those who die having never embraced Christ or the scriptural teaching on what is neces-sary to have eternal life with God? Where do they go, if any-where? Is it a painful place? Is it permanent? I will warn you now: this is not going to be a fun chapter to read, but I will try to keep it short and to the point. Jesus himself is going to tell us that we need to hear this truth now, not later.

- *What happens to me if I die with Christ?*

  What about those who truly embraced the gospel

message and met the requirements in this life to have an eternal relationship with God? Where do they go after death, if anywhere? What will it be like? Is it permanent? For many of you, great comfort will be found in what you will read, but it may be very different from the mental model you currently have. You will definitely not want to stop reading after this chapter. The best is yet to come.

- *What happens to me if I don't know Christ when he returns?*

This chapter is likely the saddest chapter I have ever written, but it is truth from Scripture and serves a very important purpose now. It is a must-read for all followers of Jesus and should have a profound impact on how you live out the rest of your days on this earth. As I studied, I discovered at least two possible endings for these folks that fall well within the realm of historical Christianity. I will present both and let you decide. Neither is a great option, but one is clearly more comforting to me than the other.

- *What happens to me if I do know Christ when he returns?*

This chapter is composed of, without question, my most favorite words I have ever written. It is this chapter where the full promise and inheritance of Christ resides. The truths in this chapter turned my gloom into glee, my doubt into a declaration, my regrets into a new resolve, my hurt into hope. This is the stuff most of us miss when the afterlife is discussed or that goes completely over our heads, or possibly isn't even said. Or, this is the truth we have never heard.

The apostle Paul wrote these great words:

It is written:

> "What no eye has seen,
>   what no ear has heard,
> and what no human mind has conceived"—
>   the things God has prepared for those who love him—
> these are the things God has revealed to us by his Spirit.
>
> —1 CORINTHIANS 2:9–10

What's next? God has revealed it to us through his Word and through his Spirit.

UNTIL THEN

Once we have a picture of "what's next," we will turn our attention to "What now?" How should we live today based on the truths of what is yet to come? The promises of God for tomorrow should dramatically affect how we all go about each day left in this body. Ours should be a purposeful life, a peaceful life, a hope-filled life. We are called to start living today as we will for all eternity. How does life get any better than that?

Maybe you have lost someone you deeply love and miss, as I did, and you want to know where he or she is. Maybe you are faced with an illness or circumstance that threatens to take your life, and you are scared. Maybe you're completely healthy right now, but you ponder the inevitable and would like to turn in your worry for a little hope and anticipation. I don't want you to wait until you get to the end of the book to know this. What I found is likely very different from what you have ever thought, or may have been taught, and (listen carefully) is so much better than you ever imagined. What God has prepared for those who know him is beautifully breathtaking.

How has it affected me, honestly? Well, as I write this, I have just gotten back from a morning doctor's appointment. Actually, it was a biopsy on a tumor on my thyroid. I won't know the full results for a few days, but I find myself in a very different place today than I did back in December 1999. I have a few jitters, but Jesus and what I have learned about our eternal life have overcome these. I still have a few questions, but today I have more answers. My heart rate rises a little when I consider the unknown, but it comes back down to near-normal range as I ponder the promise of what's to come.

This assurance from Jesus has been fulfilled in my life: "You will know the truth, and the truth will set you free" (John 8:32). I pray you receive this same gift as you read.

CHAPTER ONE

Is Jesus Enough?

HANGING ON TO LIFE BY A THREAD, MY MOM ASKED me, "Is Jesus enough?"

When she'd prayed the Sinner's Prayer years before, she had acknowledged her sins; confessed that Jesus is the Son of God, who died and rose again on the third day; and requested that his work on the cross be applied as payment for her sins, to grant her a relationship with God that would last for all eternity. But at age sixty-two, with only three days more on this earth, she honestly asked her pastor-son if this decision and prayer was enough to get her to heaven.

My instant answer to her, as I shared in the introduction, was, "Why, of course, Mom!" But truthfully, I harbored some uncertainty in the back of my mind.

Could salvation really be as simple as receiving a gift, particularly a gift you do not deserve? Grace is such a mind-boggling concept. No other area of life gives so much and requires so little from the recipient. This might be one of those "too good to be true" offers—make sure you read the fine print; there must be a catch.

1

On top of that, there is that handful of scriptures that give us pause, such as "Faith without deeds is dead" (James 2:26). Faith is one part of the equation, sure, but so are good works. Now the question becomes, how many good works are enough? Or does God grade on a curve, comparing my works with yours?

In the past, I had laid side by side the steps in the process—or the formula, if you will—for how to obtain eternal life, as taught by each of the major denominations and expressions of Christianity. I considered the doctrine of the Lutherans, the Church of Christ, the Baptists, the Catholics, the Methodists, the Presbyterians, and the Reformed folks. Each church has its own opinion about the particulars.

Take baptism, for example. Some churches embrace the baptism of an infant, while others accept baptism only after one has personally made the decision to accept Jesus as Savior. Some are comfortable with sprinkling water on the recipient, while others demand full immersion in the water. Some baptize the individual backward in the water in the name of Jesus; others baptize the candidate forward three times in the name of the Father, the Son, and the Holy Spirit.

Some see baptism as a step of obedience but not an act required to receive salvation; others see baptism as the essential act to secure one's salvation. Some groups believe the person who ultimately embraces Christ was elected in advance by God to receive salvation; other groups believe the decision is completely a matter of free will available to all. The list goes on and on.

While there seems to be an unlimited number of theological nuances in the process of receiving God's salvation, I noticed a

2

very strong spine they all had in common: Jesus. No one seemed to struggle with Acts 4:12: "Salvation is found in no one else, for there is no other name under heaven given to mankind by which we must be saved." At the end of the day, no one comes into a relationship with God without the work of Jesus Christ on the cross. The steps may differ from denomination to denomination, but at the core it is Jesus alone who saves us. This is a very helpful foundation from which to start.

But then there were those certain other passages of the Bible that had always bothered me—passages that seemed to challenge the notion that salvation is as simple as receiving a free gift. They seemed to say that works and perseverance have to be involved to solidify the transaction. In my early years of sitting in church, or even in college and seminary, the teachers of the denomination I was involved with simply pontificated with confidence that faith was enough. Feeling somewhat inferior to their intellectual prowess and years invested in study at the time, I shrugged my shoulders and hoped for the best. As long as death seemed a long way off, it was really an easy topic to ignore.

But not now. My mom was in grave danger, and I needed truth.

Over those next three days, I went to the Scriptures with a hurting heart and an open mind to discover the truth about salvation while there was still time. I had no interest in defending any denomination's position or in sugarcoating things for an upcoming funeral. This was a pure matter of life and death for someone I cared about so deeply that tears still come to my eyes writing about her now, fifteen years later.

I wasn't super interested in secondary passages that implicitly

3

addressed the question of what it really takes to secure eternal life; I wanted to study the passages that explicitly provided the answer. When we come to the end of our days, is Jesus really enough? Does faith in him plus nothing else make us right with God?

These are questions we all need to dig into more deeply at some point in our faith journeys. We often are tempted to gloss over passages we can't explain or that cause us consternation, but that simply puts up a false front of confidence and leaves a damaging niggling in the back of our minds that becomes full-blown doubt when difficult circumstances arise. So let's walk a different path here and dive into some of those tensions and difficult passages together.

MARK 10:17–22

As we step into this story, we find Jesus in the heart of his ministry. People were swarming him from all sides for just a touch that might heal them, just a word that might free them from bondage. As he entered into the region of Judea, a rich young ruler approached him with our very question. Here's how the story begins to unfold:

> As Jesus started on his way, a man ran up to him and fell on his knees before him. "Good teacher," he asked, "what must I do to inherit eternal life?"
>
> —MARK 10:17

The rich man asked the $64,000 question (although the answer will prove to be worth much more than that): "What must

4

I do?" or, in essence, "What's it going to take? How do I make sure I get to heaven? What is the key, the answer, the secret?"

In classic Jesus style, he asked the man another question before answering his inquiry. Jesus was a genius at getting people to think. People learn best in a dialogue versus a monologue—"talk with me, not at me"—and Jesus engaged them by following their questions with questions that prompted thought about issues at play that they possibly hadn't even considered. He was revealing the answer to the rich man's inquiry through the question he asked in return.

"Why do you call me good?" Jesus answered. "No one is good— except God alone. You know the commandments: 'You shall not murder, you shall not commit adultery, you shall not steal, you shall not give false testimony, you shall not defraud, honor your father and mother.'"

"Teacher," he declared, "all these I have kept since I was a boy."

Jesus looked at him and loved him. "One thing you lack," he said. "Go, sell everything you have and give to the poor, and you will have treasure in heaven. Then come, follow me."

At this the man's face fell. He went away sad, because he had great wealth.

—MARK 10:18–22

Jesus wasn't trying to stump the guy or yank his chain. On the contrary, the passage says that Jesus looked at him and loved him. He really wanted the young ruler to get it. The answer seems straightforward from the very lips of Jesus. You want to inherit life with God? Do good works.

What? Isn't this contrary to everything we've been taught about grace? This is not the good news we've heard about Jesus; this is bad news, especially for those who are nearing the end, as my mother was when she voiced her lingering question. She had no time left to do any more good works. She certainly wasn't wealthy like the rich young ruler, but neither did she sell all she did have and give it to the poor. Neither have I, for that matter.

Was Jesus really saying that the key to inheriting eternal life is through an impossibly high standard of good works? Have we been mistaken all this time? If so, if this is the truth, let's face it head-on and get to work!

But before we strap on our tool belts and empty our bank accounts, let's look at the next passage that immediately comes to mind to compare and contrast its message with this teaching of Jesus.

EPHESIANS 2:8–9

Unlike any other organization at the time when Paul wrote the book of Ephesians, the church in Ephesus was made up of Jews and Gentiles coming together to form one unified body of Christ—or at least that was the intent. Racism then was as strong, if not stronger, than it is now, and the Jews and the Gentiles could not have been more different from each other. On top of that, the Jews really wanted to add some extra steps to the salvation process that required Gentiles to do some things they did as Jews, such as being circumcised and observing certain dietary restrictions.

But Paul was seeking to tear down the walls dividing the

church and to unify them around the truth of the gospel message they should all embrace together. Without mincing words, he clearly and simply laid out the formula for eternal life for both the Jews and the Gentiles:

> For it is by grace you have been saved, through faith—and this is not from yourselves, it is the gift of God—not by works, so that no one can boast.

The path to eternal life, to being saved? *Grace.* It's a word that simply means we didn't earn it. The decision to make a way for us to have an eternal relationship with God is a gift. Read the entire second chapter of Ephesians, and you will clearly see the gift Paul refers to is Jesus' death as payment for our sins on the cross. Why do we need this payment? We all are imperfect and thus cannot come before a just God, but when Jesus, God in human form, who was innocent of all sin, died on the cross, he took the punishment we all deserved. His blood was the payment, the cost of admission for us to stand in the presence of God. It is the only sufficient payment for our sins. And the means by which we reach out and receive this gift is "through faith," understanding the deal God is offering us and trusting in it as the pathway to salvation.

What, then, must we do to gain eternal life? Place our faith in Christ.

The part that seemingly comes into conflict with Jesus' words to the rich young ruler in Mark 10 is where Paul goes on to make it clear that salvation is "not by works." If Paul had left this last phrase out, we could simply combine the two concepts together:

Faith (accepting God's gift) + Works (doing good)
= Salvation (eternal life, heaven, etc.)

But instead, Paul overtly declared that works contribute nothing to a person's salvation. So how do we reconcile this seeming contradiction?

JOHN 3:16

Let's take a look at another teaching of Jesus, found in arguably the most popular verse in the Bible.

For God so loved the world that he gave his one and only Son, that whoever believes in him shall not perish but have eternal life.

How does one take hold of eternal life? Believe in Jesus.

To ensure we don't misunderstand, Jesus repeated himself numerous times. (The emphasis in the following verses is mine.)

- "Whoever *believes* in the Son has eternal life, but whoever rejects the Son will not see life, for God's wrath remains on them" (John 3:36).
- "Very truly I tell you, whoever hears my word and *believes* him who sent me has eternal life and will not be judged but has crossed over from death to life" (John 5:24).
- "For my Father's will is that everyone who looks to the Son and *believes* in him shall have eternal life, and I will raise them up at the last day" (John 6:40).

8

- "Very truly I tell you, the one who *believes* has eternal life" (John 6:47).

Clearly, Jesus agrees with Paul. So what was he really saying to the rich young ruler when he gave him a list of rules to keep?

Consider this: He wasn't telling the guy to keep the law perfectly but was asking him to admit he couldn't keep the law perfectly. Jesus wanted him to give in and confess that eternal life was not within his power or ability. He was trying to get him to say, "I can't, but you can."

Remember when the man called Jesus "good teacher"? Jesus immediately replied, "Why do you call me good? No one is good—except God alone" (Mark 10:17–18). What point was Jesus making?

1. Only God is good.
2. By calling me good, you are unknowingly revealing that I am no mere human.

If the young, proud, self-sufficient man had humbled himself and said, "I can't," Jesus would have gone on to tell him what he told everyone else: "Yes, it is true that you are not able, but I am. Believe in me, and you will have eternal life." But this was too big a step for the proud young man to make. So, he walked away.

For those of us willing to concede that we are not able, though, and that we need Jesus' help, what follows is another crucial question: "How do I believe?" or in other words, "How do I place my faith in Christ?" This leads us to our next no-nonsense, give-it-to-me-straight passage.

ROMANS 10:9–10

If you declare with your mouth, "Jesus is Lord," and believe in your heart that God raised him from the dead, you will be saved. For it is with your heart that you believe and are justified, and it is with your mouth that you profess your faith and are saved.

Paul gave us a simple, two-step process:

Step 1: Believe in your heart.
Step 2: Profess it with your mouth.

There must be an inward decision and an outward declaration. Believing something from the heart means more than understanding it in your head. With regard to salvation, it means your mind has understood Christ's offer of grace and sent it to the heart, the executive center of your life, for a decision. When the heart believes, essentially it means your will fully embraces and trusts in the idea. What idea?

- That we can't earn our salvation through good works
- That Jesus' death on the cross provides full payment for our sins—past, present, and future
- That Jesus' resurrection from the dead authenticates he is no ordinary man but is God
- That embracing these truths is the only pathway to eternal life with God

Paul said it starts in the heart, an inward decision, but there is one more step. We must declare it out loud with our mouths. We must profess publicly this inward decision. Jesus himself said:

> What good is it for someone to gain the whole world, and yet lose or forfeit their very self? Whoever is ashamed of me and my words, the Son of Man will be ashamed of them when he comes in his glory and in the glory of the Father and of the holy angels.
>
> —LUKE 9:25–26

In Peter's first sermon, he clearly expressed the same two-step process. After telling the story of Jesus from beginning to end, laying out all that had led to Jesus' crucifixion and resurrection, Peter wrapped up his stirring message with these words:

> "Therefore let all Israel be assured of this: God has made this Jesus, whom you crucified, both Lord and Messiah."
>
> When the people heard this, they were cut to the heart and said to Peter and the other apostles, "Brothers, what shall we do?"
>
> Peter replied, "Repent and be baptized, every one of you, in the name of Jesus Christ for the forgiveness of your sins. And you will receive the gift of the Holy Spirit."
>
> —ACTS 2:36–38

When the crowd asked what they needed to do, Peter offered two specific steps: (1) repent and (2) be baptized.

Repenting is the inward decision. The word *repent* means to do a 180-degree turn, to recognize you were going in the wrong direction. As Isaiah the prophet said, "We all, like sheep, have gone astray, each of us has turned to our own way" (Isaiah 53:6). Once you've recognized your misdirection, you abandon your course and start heading in a new direction, toward God and his kingdom. Repentance is not just an intellectual acknowledgment of your mistake, but also a decision with the intent to live differently.

> REPENTANCE IS NOT JUST AN INTELLECTUAL ACKNOWLEDGMENT OF YOUR MISTAKE, BUT ALSO A DECISION WITH THE INTENT TO LIVE DIFFERENTLY.

Baptism, as a further step, is the outward declaration, the public profession of this inward decision to turn to God. Whatever the form of baptism—sprinkling or immersion—the event is intended to be a public declaration. When new converts were baptized in a public pool of water in the first century, people from the community, not just the church folks, lined the banks. They witnessed this external demonstration of allegiance to Jesus. It became public record. If you were accused of being a Christian and taken to court in those days of persecution, this evidence would declare you guilty beyond a reasonable doubt.

Different expressions within the Christian faith use different words and ways to express this inward decision and outward declaration, but I believe, in the end, God looks at a person's heart. One can fulfill all the steps of catechism and say all the right words; go through the motions of taking communion every week for one's entire life to receive God's grace; and even be baptized by sprinkling or in a church baptistery or in the Jordan River; but if the heart has not genuinely embraced Jesus, the authenticity of the redemption transaction is in question. Only God can peer into the heart to see if the decision was truly genuine.

I have been personally connected to three different denominations during my forty-year journey with Jesus. Each group brands their process as the right way. Personally, I'm a little worn out by these claims. If there was just one way to express your inward decision and outward declaration, the writers of the Bible would, in my opinion, have been morally obligated to proclaim it consistently. Many parts of the world only have a small portion of the Bible translated into their languages. Can you imagine these folks getting to the judgment seat only to find they'd had the wrong section the whole time?

Bottom line: God looks at our hearts' decisions!

There are many things in the Bible that are a little difficult to understand, but this isn't one of them. God has made the path clear. Eternal life with God does not come by our own works but by the grace of God as a gift through the person and work of Jesus Christ. We must receive this gift by placing our trust in Christ, through believing in him and what he has done for us. We do this when we inwardly make this choice in our hearts and then outwardly profess this inward decision to the world.

The only question remaining is whether we will take this step of faith. Will we swallow our pride and admit we can't get to heaven on our own? Or will we respond as the rich young ruler did? Will we stop trying to earn God's favor and accept his unbelievable grace? Will we have the courage to profess our decision out loud so our family, friends, neighbors, coworkers, and fellow students clearly know that we belong to Jesus? Will we humble ourselves in front of others and have a pastor pour water on our heads, or be dunked into a pool or river of water, to demonstrate our devotion to Jesus and proclaim that our old life has been buried with him in his death and we now have new life in him through his resurrection?

Jesus said, "You study the Scriptures diligently because you think that in them you have eternal life. These are the very Scriptures that testify about me, yet you refuse to come to me to have life" (John 5:39–40). The truth is there; the truth is clear. The way to eternal life in Jesus was laid out clearly in the Old Testament but is even more in your face in the New Testament. Will you choose to receive it, or to refuse it? Or, put differently, will you choose to receive Jesus, or to refuse him?

I went back to my mom's hospital room to share this confident discovery with her. By this time she was sedated from the pain medications, but the nurse told me that my mom could still hear and understand me. So I leaned down and whispered into her ear, "Mom, I double-checked to make sure, and I just want you to know that it is enough. Christ is enough! You can let go now; I will be right behind you."

Truth is, my mom was afraid of dying. She never really got connected to a church, and that lack of connection to Christ's community stunted her growth and robbed her of the assurance of her salvation. To this day her fear and uncertainty has been one of the hardest things to see on the face of someone I loved so deeply. But the important thing was that she believed in her heart and professed with her mouth Jesus as her Lord. And that was enough.

Enough

Recently, I gave the content of this chapter in a message to the people I serve in San Antonio, Texas. What I didn't know was that a beautiful, sixty-eight-year-old lady named Lynda Coe was in attendance. She had battled depression and bipolar disorder, ignited by her experience with postpartum depression after the birth of her son. Her daughter-in-law wrote this about Lynda in her blog:

> She battled her entire life from a pit of despair. She also struggled with alcoholism. These two combinations were a recipe that no one enjoyed facing. The struggle was real for everyone in the family. There were many apologies and broken promises along the way.[1]

In an attempt to provide help and healing, Lynda's daughter, Shar, invited her to Oak Hills Church, where I am privileged to minister. Not too many visits in, Lynda found herself sitting in the service as I was sharing this story about my mother. I made the point as passionately as I could that "Christ is enough." Lynda, it turned out, was not only listening but was taking copious notes.

In fact, the last line she wrote and embraced was "Christ is all u need."

Four days later Lynda passed away.

15

But because she embraced this message from her heart, she discovered what my mom discovered the moment she exhaled her last breath: eternal life with God is real, and all it requires is simple faith in Jesus and a declaration of that faith.

I say the same thing to you right now that I told my mom and Lynda Coe: "Jesus is enough!"

If you have never made this inward decision from your heart, let me invite you to say to God the same prayer I prayed when I was fourteen, the same one my mom prayed when she was forty-one, and the same one Lynda Coe prayed when she was sixty-eight.

Dear Father in heaven,

I know I am a sinner, and I ask for your forgiveness. I know that I can't save myself, but you can save me. I believe that your Son, Jesus Christ, died for my sins and rose from the dead. I trust and follow you as my Lord and Savior. Guide my life and help me to do your will.

In Jesus' name, amen

If you prayed this prayer for the first time, you now need to declare it with your mouth. Tell everybody. Find a Bible-believing church in your area, and ask them to guide you in the way to outwardly demonstrate your inward decision to trust Christ.

Would you allow me to be one of the first to whom you profess your faith out loud? Here is my e-mail address: randyf@oakhillschurch.com.

I promise to pray for you personally.

16

LIFE IN BETWEEN

CHAPTER TWO

What Happens If
I Die Without Christ?

A BUSINESSMAN, WHILE AWAY ON VACATION, WAS reading his hometown newspaper. He was stunned to come across his own obituary. Shocked and angered, he immediately called the editor on the telephone.

"I'm calling about the report of my death in your paper yesterday!" he exclaimed.

"Yes, sir," came the reply. "And from where might you be calling?"

Good question. Where exactly do we go after we exhale our last breath?

I recently discovered that there are 2,667 death cafés in thirty-two countries around the world. *What are death cafés?* you may be wondering. Death cafés are forums where people gather around a cup of joe to discuss death.[1] Obviously, there is a certain amount of morbid fascination with the topic of death, possibly because of the mystery surrounding the passing from this life to the next, but

19

I have a hunch that people are actually less interested in death and more interested in life after death. Wouldn't you agree?

Where exactly do our souls end up after we die? The Bible clearly teaches there are two options. In this chapter, we'll deal with the first destination and answer the question, what happens to me if I die without Christ? Let's get started.

THE THREE STAGES

To answer this question it might be helpful to first lay out a framework of what the Bible teaches as the three stages of life:

- Life Now
- Life In Between
- Life Forever

Life Now

Let's start with Life Now. This is the stage you are in even as you read this book. It's the time between conception in your mother's womb and death. The length of this time varies from person to person. The longest human life we know of is recorded in Genesis 5:27. The Bible says, "Altogether, Methuselah lived a total of 969 years, and then he died." Currently, the average life span of men of all races in America is 76.4 years, and 81.2 years for American women.[2] Why do women live longer than men? We can only speculate, but should you choose to hypothesize about the answer to that question, be careful whom you share your answer with. You just might meet your Maker at that time.

But seriously, in the overall scheme of things, Life Now is really rather insignificant in comparison with what is still to come. Whether you live one day or 969 years, both expanses pale in comparison with eternity.

Life In Between

When a person dies, his or her body is buried, and his or her spirit moves from Life Now to Life In Between. In theological writings this stage is called "the intermediate state." Something important you need to know, which may surprise you, is that the Old Testament has very little to say about the afterlife, or what we're calling "Life In Between," and the New Testament only has a few verses about this second stage. I hate to tell you, but all the sermons and pontificating you have heard about the pearly gates, streets of gold, and so forth, well, we're not quite there yet in the timeline of what happens directly after death. All of that doesn't come into play until the third stage, Life Forever. But for now, we're focusing on Life In Between.

Jesus himself gave us the best look at Life In Between in the story of the rich man and Lazarus:

> There was a rich man who was dressed in purple and fine linen and lived in luxury every day. At his gate was laid a beggar named Lazarus, covered with sores and longing to eat what fell from the rich man's table. Even the dogs came and licked his sores.
>
> The time came when the beggar died and the angels carried him to Abraham's side. The rich man also died and was buried. In Hades, where he was in torment, he looked up and

saw Abraham far away, with Lazarus by his side. So he called to him, "Father Abraham, have pity on me and send Lazarus to dip the tip of his finger in water and cool my tongue, because I am in agony in this fire."

But Abraham replied, "Son, remember that in your lifetime you received your good things, while Lazarus received bad things, but now he is comforted here and you are in agony. And besides all this, between us and you a great chasm has been set in place, so that those who want to go from here to you cannot, nor can anyone cross over from there to us."

—LUKE 16:19–26

Two men died—a rich man and a beggar. Their bodies were buried in the ground, and Life Now came to an end for both of them. Their spirits—some might say their souls—went to the same place, which is divided into two compartments, the upper and the lower, with a chasm between them. Here is a super simple drawing that represents the picture Jesus was painting for us.

Jesus referred to the lower compartment, where the rich man ended up, as "Hades." He referred to the upper compartment, where Lazarus ended up, as "Abraham's side." Other translations refer to that upper compartment as "Abraham's bosom." We are not really sure where this in-between place is located, but we do know this is where the spirits of the dead, both believers and unbelievers, go after their bodies give out. It is important to note here that

Abraham's Side

Chasm

Hades

22

after the death and resurrection of Christ, there is a shift in residence for believers. We will cover that more in the next chapter.

SHEOL, HADES, HELL, AND THE BLACKEST DARKNESS

What happens to a person who dies today without ever accepting the forgiveness of sins through the shed blood of Jesus? That individual's body goes into the grave, and his or her spirit goes to Hades—a holding place where the person awaits the final judgment yet to come.

It's certainly not a pretty picture . . . or at least not one any of us would choose. When I accepted Christ more than forty years ago, I must admit I did so mostly because the pastor "scared the Hades out of me." I wasn't raised in a Christian home and didn't go to church until at the age of fourteen I was invited by a neighbor two doors down.

The church my neighbor took me to was one of those "hellfire and brimstone" kind of churches. There I didn't so much hear what God was saving me for; I only heard about what God was saving me from—the fiery pit of hell, where there is weeping, wailing, and gnashing of teeth. This scared the bejeebers out of me! But I'm pretty sure there is more to the story than the snippet I was exposed to back then.

God has a different, fuller vision for us than simply escaping the flames. His vision is not so much to save us *from* death as it is to save us *for* life. It's not so much to save us *from* hell as it is to save us *for* life with him.

This is one of the hardest things to wrap your mind around, and some people can never accept that. This lack of acceptance is the reason we're talking about Hades now.

So what is the full truth? What is hell like? And is hell the same thing as Hades?

Let's start with this last question. In the Old Testament the primary word used to refer to the place one goes to at death is *sheol*. Most of the time it simply refers to the abode of the dead, both the righteous and the wicked (Job 17:13; Psalm 16:10; Isaiah 38:10).

Interestingly, the Greek translation of the Old Testament, called the Septuagint, translates *sheol* with the Greek word *Hades*. In fact, *Hades* is virtually synonymous with *sheol* throughout the Old Testament. How did Hades, which was once a term that referred to the holding place for both the righteous and the wicked who had passed away, become more widely known as a place of punishment? Jesus further developed the idea in the New Testament, starting with the Luke 16 story, by referring to Hades primarily as the temporary dwelling place of the wicked who had died instead of the place where both the righteous and the wicked went.[3]

All ten times the word *Hades* is used in the New Testament, the King James Version, also known as the Authorized Version, translates it "hell." So, the words *Hades* and *hell*, beginning in the New Testament, refer to the same place: the temporary dwelling place of the spirits of those who died without Christ.

What is this place like? Some scholars don't think Hades, or hell, is an actual place of fire. It's kind of difficult for a spirit to feel the effects of fire. It would seem you'd need a body for that. Perhaps there is a burning sensation the spirit can feel that results in a tormenting experience. But in the end, we really just don't know for sure. What we do know is that this is a place to avoid at all costs.

Jude 13 refers to it as a place of "blackest darkness." I don't know about you, but that simply terrifies me. I am a night-light kind of guy. The winter, with its shorter days, is my least favorite time of the year. I sigh with satisfaction when the sun hits my face. Anywhere that is in perpetual darkness is at the top of the list of places I want to avoid.

But the worst part of all is not the darkness or the actual torment but the sense of solitary confinement from God's presence and the knowledge of pending judgment. Second Thessalonians 1:9 tells us that those who do not know God "will suffer the punishment of eternal destruction, away from the presence of the Lord and from the glory of his might" (ESV). It will be like waking up every day on death row, with no chance of a stay of execution. In essence, Hades is banishment from the very presence of God and the life we were made to live while we await our final judgment. Certainly not the end to the story any of us would want.

THE CHOICE TO BE MADE DURING LIFE NOW

Why is this even a potential end to any of our stories? Where did it all begin? Banishment from the presence of God began when Adam and Eve rejected God's vision for their life together with him in the garden and ate the forbidden fruit. This is what Genesis 3:23–24 tells us happened:

25

So the LORD God banished him from the Garden of Eden. . . . After he drove the man out, he placed on the east side of the Garden of Eden cherubim and a flaming sword flashing back and forth to guard the way to the tree of life.

This was the beginning of humanity's separation from God, the first hint of Hades. The day before, Adam and Eve had been taking walks with God in the cool of the day. Now they were banished from his presence and the amazing life he had envisioned for them. And the same would be true for all who came after them, including you and me.

If no resolution is made to our sin condition before our physical bodies die (i.e., renewal through acceptance of Christ's offer for forgiveness), banishment from God's presence must continue for our spirits, which live on. This is what we've been calling "Hades" or "hell."

What I am about to tell you is uber important: *this decision of banishment was not God's will.* This decision was the will of Adam and Eve when they disobeyed God and ate from the forbidden tree. Their decision to eat this particular fruit was not to curb hunger pangs. They had many fruit trees in the garden to choose from. This was their way of telling God they rejected him as their God and wanted to be gods of their own. Adam and Eve swallowed Satan's lie about God's goodness and took things into their own hands. Once their teeth sank into the first bite of the fruit, everything changed. Sin entered into their lives, making them unfit to live in community with God. This led to their exile from the garden.

The same is true for you and for me. It may seem a bit unfair,

26

but we weren't given the same opportunity as Adam and Eve. They started out sinless and chose to sin; we start out already in sin because their sin virus is transferred to us at conception. We verify the presence of this spiritual disease in our souls when we deliberately choose to sin against God or people, something we all unfortunately do at one point or another. As a result, we all live in a state of broken relationship because of our sins, thus the gulf between us and the holy and righteous God. But when Christ came and offered himself as a sacrifice to bear the weight of our sins and make us right before God, he opened the door to a new choice.

God now turns to you and says, "I have provided the way for you to come back into the garden—Paradise!—and live with me. Do you want to be there?" Just as Adam had a choice to embrace a relationship with God or to walk away from it, so you have a choice to make.

Consider this truth: *God doesn't send anyone to hell; he merely honors a person's choice.*

True love does not force another to love him back. God is pure love. He loves you enough to have given his one and only Son to provide a way back into a relationship with him. He simply wants to know how you feel about him. He will honor your decision.

C. S. Lewis, well-known author, Oxford professor, apologist, and philosopher, said:

GOD DOESN'T SEND ANYONE TO HELL; HE MERELY HONORS A PERSON'S CHOICE.

I willingly believe that the damned are, in one sense, successful, rebels to the end; that the doors of hell are locked on the *inside* . . . They enjoy forever the horrible freedom they have demanded, and are therefore self-enslaved: just as the blessed, forever submitting to obedience, become through all eternity more and more free.[4]

You have a choice to make. God has made the way to eternal life possible through faith in Christ. Remember, as we discovered together in the last chapter, Jesus is enough! He wants you to want him and the life he always intended for you to live. But he won't hold a cosmic gun to your head. Let's go back and look at the rest of the story of the rich man and Lazarus.

> He [the rich man] answered, "Then I beg you, father, send Lazarus to my family, for I have five brothers. Let him warn them, so that they will not also come to this place of torment."
>
> Abraham replied, "They have Moses and the Prophets; let them listen to them."
>
> "No, father Abraham," he said, "but if someone from the dead goes to them, they will repent."
>
> He said to him, "If they do not listen to Moses and the Prophets, they will not be convinced even if someone rises from the dead."
>
> —LUKE 16:27–31

I have to admit, I kind of agree with the rich guy. In my opinion, it would be extremely effective for a person to come back from the dead, not just a near-death experience, and stand before people who knew him and say, "Here's what awaits you on the other side." That would get my attention. How about yours?

But Abraham said, "No, Moses and the Prophets are enough." When he used the phrase "Moses and the Prophets," he was referring to the Old Testament Scriptures. They alone are enough to point us to Christ and faith in God for salvation, but now we have the New Testament as well. We have the whole story as God has revealed it, and it tells us the whole truth.

Think about it. There was a person who died and three days later came back to life and stood before hundreds of people who knew him. Some believed; most did not. If the resurrection of Jesus from the dead doesn't work for you, certainly the resurrection of Lazarus won't either.

Today believers in Jesus have all the keys they need to open the gates to the kingdom of heaven—the truth about Jesus and salvation revealed in Scripture. But as I have already stated, God won't force himself on you. You have to choose to accept the sacrifice Jesus made when he died on the cross to cover your sins. You need to ask for that forgiveness to be applied to you. Have you called out and asked Jesus to forgive you and save you, not so much to save you from hell and banishment from his presence but to save you for life with him as he intended from the beginning?

It's a surprisingly simple process to say, "Yes, God, I choose you." Often we almost want it to be more difficult. But salvation cannot be found in something you do. And that is Jesus' point. The rich man's accomplishments and works and riches did him no good in Life In Between. Meanwhile, Lazarus, whose name means "God, the Helper," relied on God alone and ended up at Abraham's side. Lazarus didn't enter paradise because of his good works or simply because he was poor; he was there because he had leaned fully into the mercy and help of God, which is the essence of the gospel. None of us can do this on our own, but God will help us get there if we truly want it.

This is a decision that must be made in Life Now. We can't opt out of the decision, because no decision is basically a decision of rejection. Sadly, this seems to be where most people I know reside. They do not openly reject Jesus' offer; they simply ignore it. But if you reject or ignore Christ's offer, God will honor your choice not to reach out to him for relationship. When you die, you will find yourself in Hades with the rich man, awaiting final judgment.

And the truth of the matter is that one day you will die. We all will. As Hebrews 9:27 says, "It is appointed unto men once to die, but after this the judgment" (KJV). When that day will come for you is hard to say. Maybe it will be today, maybe tomorrow, maybe fifty years from now. But the big question, regardless, is, when your obituary is recorded in the local newspaper and you want to make a comment on what was written, from where will you be calling?

The choice is yours to make.

CHAPTER THREE

What Happens If
I Die with Christ?

MY FIRST EXPERIENCE WITH WATERSKIING CAME AT age twenty-four. I was quietly anxious about the adventure. All my focus was on getting up on those skis.

The first attempt was over before it began. One tug from the motorboat, and the rope left my hands and took off without me. On the second try, I got up for a brief second before I face-planted and a rush of brown lake water was sent up my nose. On the third attempt I kept the tension just right to bring my body out of the water. As my body fully emerged, I leaned back just a bit and found the slot. I did it! I was water-skiing. A smile overtook my entire face. I had accomplished the goal! Check.

Then it dawned on me. I had spent all my energy and focus on my entrance strategy and had invested zero time considering my exit strategy. I had no idea how to end this experience. Fear overtook me. Thoughts of my falling body skipping across the water

31

like a smooth stone came to mind. A vision of my legs rising above my head as I made contact with the concrete water below elevated my blood pressure.

So I held on for dear life as the boat continued circling the small lake. The guys on the boat began to yell out something to me, but I couldn't quite make it out. By this time my hands and legs were cramping. How was this going to end? It had to end. I couldn't hold on forever. I yelled for the guys to speak louder.

They screamed at the tops of their lungs, "Let go of the rope!"

Let go of the rope? They must be insane. What happens to a body that just lets go of the rope and gives up? I didn't know, because I had never experienced it before. I doubled down on my grip and kept skiing, completely unsure of how it was all eventually going to end.

Life is so often like my waterskiing adventure. We use all our energy getting up and staying up but don't have an exit strategy. We know we can't continue the ride forever in this body—it will eventually give out—but because we don't know how the ride ends and fear it will hurt, we hold on for dear life. Woody Allen wrote, "I don't mind dying; I just don't want to be there when it happens."[1] Boy, can I relate!

What is the exit strategy for the Christian? If I say yes to Christ in this life, what happens to me when I die, when I let go of the rope?

Recall from our last chapter that there are three stages in life:

- Life Now—from conception to death
- Life In Between—from death to the return of Christ
- Life Forever—from the return of Christ to eternity

32

When a person, believer in Jesus or not, dies, he or she moves to the second stage, Life In Between. It is not the final destination but one we all must go through. We have already laid out the horrible path for the person who fails to receive the gift of forgiveness in this life. Essentially, that individual's body goes into the ground while his or her spirit goes into a holding tank called Hades, awaiting the final judgment. This person should be highly motivated to hold on for dear life in this body, because the next two stages are devastating.

But what happens to the person who does receive the once-and-for-all forgiveness of sins through Jesus? Truthfully, the Bible doesn't say a whole lot about it beyond Jesus' parable about the rich man and Lazarus. The Old Testament is virtually silent on the topic of what happens to the godly in the stage in between death and God's ultimate redemption, and the New Testament contains just a few passages. What about the pearly gates, the streets of gold, and my mansion in heaven? you ask. Sorry. Remember: those will exist in Life Forever, but not in this stage.

FROM ABRAHAM'S SIDE TO HEAVEN

Let's take another look at Jesus' parable in Luke 16. You will recall that two men die, a rich man and Lazarus. The rich man's body is placed in the ground, and his spirit goes to Hades, or hell. Lazarus's body also is placed in the ground, and his spirit goes to a corresponding place to Hades with a chasm in between.

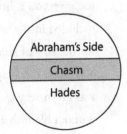

33

Hades is a place of torment, while Abraham's side is a refreshing paradise filled with peace. The chasm in between prevents travel to the other side, although the people in Hades can apparently see into Abraham's side. We are not told that the spirits in Abraham's side can see into Hades, which would make sense. It would not be very peaceful gazing into the torment, particularly if you knew someone there.

Now, keep in mind, the Bible is not particularly clear about this, but here is what I've concluded aligns with the whole story of Scripture. When we think about the afterlife, we tend to deal only with people who lived after Christ finished his work on the cross. To gain a fuller understanding, we need to factor into our mental model what happened to the millions of people who existed before Christ. Where did they go, if anywhere?

In the Old Testament and up until the crucifixion of Christ, when a person who placed his faith in God died, his body was buried in the ground and his spirit went to Abraham's side. It was a restful and peaceful place, but it was still not in the full presence of God. Why? Because the blood of the animal sacrifices, which the Israelites offered in the Old Testament for the forgiveness of their sins to make them right before God, was not sufficient.

If you are not familiar with this Old Testament practice, let me give you a little background. During the time of Moses, God included in the law the requirement of animal sacrifices as payment for the sins of Israel. The most important sacrifices took place once a year on the Day of Atonement, or Yom Kippur. The high priest was given very specific instructions on the sacrifice of male animals without blemish as an atonement or satisfactory payment for offenses or sins against the Lord. The following passage lays out the law:

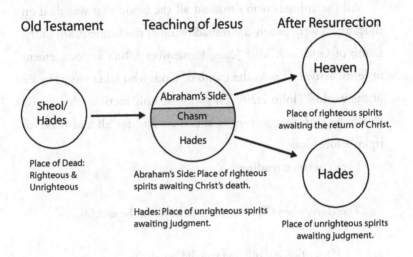

"This is to be a lasting ordinance for you: Atonement is to be made once a year for all the sins of the Israelites."

And it was done, as the LORD commanded Moses.

—LEVITICUS 16:34

Now turn to the New Testament after the crucifixion of Christ, and take a look at Hebrews 10:1–4:

The law is only a shadow of the good things that are coming— not the realities themselves. For this reason it can never, by the same sacrifices repeated endlessly year after year, make perfect those who draw near to worship. Otherwise, would they not have stopped being offered? For the worshipers would have been cleansed once for all, and would no longer have felt guilty for their sins. But those sacrifices are an annual reminder of sins. It is impossible for the blood of bulls and goats to take away sins.

All the animals who died and all the blood that was shed on those altars were merely a foreshadowing of the future death of the Lamb of God, or Christ Jesus. Remember John's announcement of Jesus' arrival, "Look, the Lamb of God, who takes away the sin of the world!" (John 1:29). This was the only sacrifice that would finally be sufficient to forgive sins once and for all and make us right before God.

Let's continue reading:

Therefore, when Christ came into the world, he said:

"Sacrifice and offering you did not desire,
 but a body you prepared for me;
with burnt offerings and sin offerings
 you were not pleased.
Then I said, 'Here I am—it is written about me in the scroll—
 I have come to do your will, my God.'"

First he said, "Sacrifices and offerings, burnt offerings and sin offerings you did not desire, nor were you pleased with them"— though they were offered in accordance with the law. Then he said, "Here I am, I have come to do your will." He sets aside the first to establish the second. And by that will, we have been made holy through the sacrifice of the body of Jesus Christ once for all.

—Hebrews 10:5–10

What is clear here is that the animal sacrifices of the Old Testament didn't fully repair the offense against God; they did not atone for the sins of believers. But until Jesus came and his blood could be applied to them, those who died could not be ushered directly into the presence of God. They had to wait. And the safe place where they waited was with the spirit of Abraham and all other believers whose bodies had died.

I believe this is the same place Jesus referred to when he was on the cross and said to the thief next to him, "Today you will be with me in paradise" (Luke 23:43).[2] He said this on a Friday, but Jesus didn't rise from the dead until Sunday. So from Friday until Sunday, Jesus and the thief had to be somewhere. Where did Jesus say they were going? Paradise.

On Friday, immediately after Jesus and the thief died, they took a journey into paradise—or Abraham's side—to retrieve all those who had died and to take them directly into the presence of God.

Can you imagine the scene? Jesus enters this place and says to all these people who have died in the past but have not had the blood of Christ applied to them yet, "My blood has been poured out and has now been applied to you. Let's get out of here!" And then Jesus takes them into the presence of God, because their sins have actually been paid for once and for all. What an incredible triumph! And this is where they all remain today—in the presence of God, or heaven.

We can't be sure this is exactly how it happened, but we can observe that following the resurrection of Jesus, the Bible stops referring to the upper chamber of sheol and only refers to the lower chamber, Hades, the place where the spirits of those who did not believe during Life Now reside—including the rich man in Jesus' story. The following illustration gives you a simple picture of the progression from the Old Testament to the New Testament.

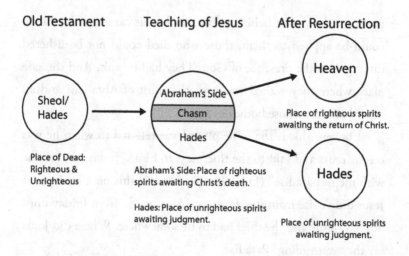

Where does the spirit of the believer in Jesus go the second after he or she dies now that Jesus has made the ultimate sacrifice? The Bible simply says our spirits go to be with the Lord. In chapter 2 we defined Life In Between for the spirits of unbelievers as banishment from the very presence of God and the life they were made to live while they await final judgment.

Here now is the biblical definition of Life In Between for the believer: being in the presence of God as we await our resurrected bodies and the life we were made to live.

Thanks be to Jesus for this wonderful gift.

"EVERYBODY WANT TO GO TO HEAVEN, BUT NOBODY WANT TO GO NOW"

As I confessed in the introduction, I embarrassingly restate here, in the spirit of Kenny Chesney's 2008 country song, "Everybody want

38

to go to heaven, but nobody want to go now"—including me.[3] The idea of my spirit exiting my body and flying up to who knows where in the atmosphere, where the air is thin and cold, doing who knows what, just leaves me a bit apprehensive, to say the least. Now, if I were suffering from chronic pain or a terminal illness, I might feel differently, but at the moment this is not my story. I know I am not alone in this. Chesney's song hit number one in the charts, signifying this is a general sentiment, at least among people who like country music.

The lack of enthusiasm for the next chapter after Life Now intensifies when coupled with *necrophobia*, or the fear of death. My mom was afraid of dying. I am afraid of dying. Sixty-eight percent of the US population is afraid of dying, a fear second only to *glossophobia*, or the fear of speaking.[4] Even the apostle Paul, in some ways, was afraid of dying, or at least saw some of what might feel disconcerting about moving from Life Now into Life In Between.

How do I, as a reverend, reconcile this seemingly *ir*reverent attitude? I have found tremendous insight and comfort from the teaching and honest confession of Paul in 2 Corinthians 4 and 5.

Paul wrote this letter to the believers who gathered in the ancient city of Corinth. At the writing of 2 Corinthians, Paul was getting older. He had been beaten for his stand for Christ. He had been imprisoned numerous times. He was plumb tired; his body was giving out. It was getting harder and harder to hold on to the rope and stay standing. And yet he did. How? By keeping his eyes focused on what he knew was yet to come. Paul looked to the end of suffering and declared that "the one who raised the Lord Jesus from the dead will also raise us with Jesus and present us with you to himself" (2 Corinthians 4:14).

Paul believed in the physical resurrection of the body of Jesus. Every believer must embrace the fact that this actually took place; otherwise, Jesus is not who he said he is—God. Paul said it was an essential part of our confession—"If you declare with your mouth, 'Jesus is Lord,' and believe in your heart that God *raised him from the dead*, you will be saved" (Romans 10:9, emphasis added).

Ephesians 1:19–20 explains that the Holy Spirit raised Jesus' dead body from the tomb, and accordingly, God promises that the Holy Spirit will also one day raise the bodies of those who believed during Life Now (1 Corinthians 15). But this will not happen for us until Life Forever. Yes, it is a glorious thing to look forward to if we keep the long-term view in mind. In fact, knowledge and belief in the resurrection of our bodies gave Paul great hope and comfort in the face of death. He wrote:

> Therefore we do not lose heart. Though outwardly we are wasting away, yet inwardly we are being renewed day by day. For our light and momentary troubles are achieving for us an eternal glory that far outweighs them all. So we fix our eyes not on what is seen, but on what is unseen, since what is seen is temporary, but what is unseen is eternal. For we know that if the earthly tent we live in is destroyed, we have a building from God, an eternal house in heaven, not built by human hands.
>
> —2 CORINTHIANS 4:16–5:1

Daily our bodies are wasting away. Can I get an "amen"? This is just a fact of life. But as we grow in Christ, Paul says, our spirits can actually get stronger. The second-best strategy for overcoming the effects of aging is diet and exercise. The first-best strategy is spiritual growth, getting healthy on the inside.

We should do everything we can to take care of our bodies (1 Corinthians 6:19–20), but eventually, time takes its toll. I am working hard to slow the process down, but I cannot stop it. I'm not only getting older, but I'm getting shorter. Somewhere between high school and now, I have lost an inch off my height. Yikes.

Death will eventually win over these perishable bodies we inherited from Adam, but as we grow spiritually and get to know God better, we will see he has a plan for us. His plan trumps all the pain and even physical death we experience in Life Now. It's a plan in which love wins and we live forever. On the day of Christ's return, we each will receive a new body, a resurrected body that is imperishable. When we fix our eyes on this promise, it makes the temporary troubles we have in Life Now seem puny in comparison. Because no matter how awful our circumstances become, we know this is not how our story ends. We will receive relief from our grief one day. The believer in Jesus can cope with this hope.

But, what about Life In Between? What about that stage most disconcerts us when we think about death and the afterlife? What Paul wrote next is very important:

> Meanwhile we groan, longing to be clothed instead with our heavenly dwelling, because when we are clothed, we will not be found naked. For while we are in this tent, we groan and are burdened, because we do not wish to be unclothed but to be clothed instead with our heavenly dwelling, so that what is mortal may be swallowed up by life. Now the one who has

fashioned us for this very purpose is God, who has given us the Spirit as a deposit, guaranteeing what is to come.

—2 CORINTHIANS 5:2–5

According to Paul, "meanwhile," as we await the return of Jesus, when we will finally receive these new bodies, we "groan." This timeline covers both Life Now, when our bodies are wasting away, and Life In Between, when our spirits leave our bodies behind. Believers long for a body that is not wasting away. We crave a body that is not facing illness or death. Can you imagine waking up tomorrow and having no fear whatsoever of ever getting sick or experiencing death? That is the grand prize for the follower of Jesus! This is the pot of gold at the end of the rainbow.

Now, what did Paul mean when he said, "For while we are in this tent, we groan and are burdened, because we do not wish to be unclothed but to be clothed instead with our heavenly dwelling"? Here is how I understand it. While we are in this "tent" (our current bodies), we live with the fear of dying, because when we die, our spirits exit our bodies and are essentially naked, without the covering or the home that was our physical bodies. This exposure and unknown experience unnerves us. I know it does me.

I hear Christians say all the time with bravado, "I am not afraid of dying." But Paul said, "I am! My spirit doesn't wish to be unclothed!" We don't have any experience or even a mental model of our spirits living outside of our bodies. I don't know about you, but I find great authenticity and freedom in joining Paul by saying, "Death freaks me out." Paul didn't look forward to dying but looked forward to his resurrected body—the new, imperishable tent for his spirit to hang out in forever. The thing is, none of us receive this new body right at the time of death but must wait until the return of Jesus to earth. Essentially, Life In Between for the believer is a time when our souls are body-less.

This in-between time can be a bit perplexing from where we are standing in Life Now. Yet we are supposed to look forward to this. It reminds me of a story I heard.

One day, an ambitious priest walked into the local tavern and said to the first man he saw, "Son, would you like to go to heaven?"

"Oh, yes, Father. I would."

"Then stand over there against that wall," the priest replied.

The man dutifully obeyed and took his place against the wall.

The priest then approached a second man. "Son," he said, "would you like to go to heaven?"

"Of course!" the man replied.

"Then stand over there against the wall," the priest told him, pointing.

Finally, the priest found a third man, seated at the bar, half drunk. "Son," he said, "would *you* like to go to heaven?"

The third man hiccupped loudly and then said, "No, sir. I–I mean, no . . . Father."

"What?!" the priest said, shocked. "Are you telling me that when you die, you really *don't* want to go to heaven?"

"Ohhhhh," the drunk slurred. "When I *die* . . . Well, yeah. Sure. I just thought you were trying to get me to go right *now*."

The truth is, we like our life now! It is all we know. So, most of us try not to think about the next life. We are glad we have a good outcome to look forward to, but we certainly don't want to be in the group going now!

How did Paul overcome this groaning burden of a fear of death and nakedness, this hesitation to want to step into Life In Between? Paul wrapped up with this strong resolution:

> Therefore we are always confident and know that as long as we are at home in the body we are away from the Lord. For we live by faith, not by sight. We are confident, I say, and would prefer to be away from the body and at home with the Lord.
>
> —2 CORINTHIANS 5:6–8

Paul got rather excited as he wrote these words and pondered what it must be like to be in the actual presence of God, even without a body. He concluded that while death is a scary thing and we don't have any firsthand experience living without bodies, being with God in spirit is still better than being away from God with a physical body. He confirmed this conviction as he wrote his letter from prison to the Philippian believers:

> For to me, to live is Christ and to die is gain. If I am to go on living in the body, this will mean fruitful labor for me. Yet what shall I choose? I do not know! I am torn between the two: I desire to depart and be with Christ, which is better by far.
>
> —PHILIPPIANS 1:21–23

Paul loved his purposeful life on earth. I totally get that. So do I. But he came to the place where he saw being away from his body and with the Lord as "better by far." If you read both of the preceding passages again, you will see his secret. He took the focus off himself and focused on being with Christ.

Consider this story:

A sick man turned to his doctor as he was preparing to leave the examination room and said, "Doctor, I am afraid to die. Tell me what lies on the other side."

Very quietly, the doctor said, "I don't know."

"You don't know? You, a Christian man, don't know what is on the other side?"

Just then, the doctor's family came for a visit and brought the family dog with them. On the other side of the closed door came the sound of scratching and whining. When the doctor opened the door to greet his family, the dog sprang into the room, leaped on the doctor, and went nuts.

Turning to the patient, the doctor said, "Did you notice my dog? He's never been in this room before. He didn't know what was on the inside. He knew nothing except that his master was there, and when the door opened, he sprang in without fear. I know little of what is on the other side of death, but I do know one thing . . . I know my Master is there, and that is enough."

What's next for believers is not so much a place as a person. We will be in the presence of God, and Paul says that is ultimately better than life in this body. Where are your loved ones

WHAT'S NEXT FOR BELIEVERS IS NOT SO MUCH A PLACE AS A PERSON. who trusted Christ in this life? There are no pearly gates or streets of gold yet. There are no mansions yet. Your departed loved ones are likely not golfing, fishing, knitting, or engaging in their favorite hobbies. We may not know much about the place of rest for Life In Between, but we do know the Person they are with. They are being held in the arms of Jesus, waiting for him to fulfill his full promise. They are alive and in a better place.

In the opening chapter I talked about my mom's death. Pancreatic cancer is one of the most brutal and painful ways to die that I have seen. It literally sucked the life out of my mom moment by moment until there was hardly anything left of her physically. Knowing that my mom is not only free of this pain and humiliation but will also never experience it again brings me great comfort. When I join her in heaven, I am not totally sure what it will be like to encounter her spirit, but I know it will be a great reunion and together we will look forward to our resurrected bodies, free from disease and death.

The same future awaits you if you put your trust in Jesus during Life Now.

Maybe you don't want to go to heaven today. That's okay. Paul agreed that the whole experience is a bit unnerving. But as you grow in your relationship with God, you will grow in your longing to be in his actual presence, as Paul did. Intimacy with God now is simply the most important and effective pursuit of your life to prepare you for the next chapter. Paul said it was for him: "I consider everything a loss because of the surpassing worth of knowing Christ Jesus my Lord" (Philippians 3:8).

46

As your body continues to fail you, you will come to see that death and what comes after is a good thing—it leads to a better place. In the meantime, don't rush it. The Bible tells us that God has numbered our days (Job 14:5; Psalm 139:16). He knows and has a good plan for your last day in that perishable body. As a believer, don't live in fear; don't lose heart. When you breathe your last breath in this body, know that you will instantaneously be ushered into the arms of Jesus.

That summer day when I was water-skiing so many years ago, I finally did it. I let go of the ski rope. What happened? My body slowly sank into the water. The life jacket kept me afloat as the boat circled around to pick me up. Everything was fine. And the next time out, I not only had an entrance strategy but an exit strategy.

Death, the Bible tells us, is a valley experience. But at some point in the valley, Jesus will meet us there and take us the rest of the way (Psalm 23:4). Death "has been swallowed up in victory" (1 Corinthians 15:54). When it is time for you to let go of the rope of life, you will discover that everything will be just fine.

No, not fine . . . better than ever.

Q&A on Life In Between

WE ALL HAVE MANY QUESTIONS ABOUT THE AFTERLIFE. The clearer our vision, the more we will anticipate what God has in store for us; and that is a good thing. Paul gives us these encouraging words:

> Brothers and sisters, we do not want you to be uninformed about those who sleep in death, so that you do not grieve like the rest of mankind, who have no hope.
>
> —1 THESSALONIANS 4:13

In the chapters you just read, I have tried to present what the Bible explicitly teaches about the afterlife, specifically that span of time between death and our ultimate restoration. Yet, often we have additional questions, the answers to which could really boost our aggregate of hope. I am seeking to meet that need here. Keep in mind the Bible doesn't always answer these additional questions explicitly, but we can draw some loosely held conclusions from what the Bible teaches implicitly.

49

Are there such things as ghosts?

Based on our English definition of the term *ghost*, the answer is yes. Webster defines *ghost* as "a disembodied soul; esp. the soul of a dead person believed to be an inhabitant of the unseen world or to appear in bodily form to living people."[1]

We already know that when we die our bodies fail but our spirits live on. By strict definition, although it is not the one I prefer, these spirits can be referred to as "ghosts." The main question at hand is whether the spirits of those who have passed on make visitations to earth after death, interacting with those still living. Overall, the Bible teaches that human spirits are in one of two places: they are either with the Lord, awaiting their bodily resurrection (2 Corinthians 5:8), or in Hades, waiting for the final judgment (Revelation 20:13). Human spirits, therefore, do not inhabit the earth and move among us, although we will discuss in a moment that we may be able to communicate with them.[2]

Apparently, the disciples believed in the concept of ghosts during their pre-resurrection relationship with Jesus. One night they were in a boat and saw a figure approaching them, walking on the water. Their first inclination was to believe it was a ghost (Matthew 14:26).[3] When Jesus appeared to the disciples after the resurrection, once again they assumed he was a ghost (Luke 24:37). John's account of this event tells us that they were meeting behind locked doors for fear of the Jews, and Jesus appeared in the room with them out of nowhere (John 20:19). Jesus responded, "Why are you troubled, and why do doubts rise in your minds? Look at my hands and my feet. It is I myself! Touch me and see; a ghost does not have flesh and bones, as you see I have" (Luke 24:38–39). If by *ghost* we are referring to a spirit, either humans or angels, then Jesus believed in them. But I am convinced that as the disciples grew in their knowledge of truth, they came to conclude that angelic spirits do exist and move among us, but human spirits, while they do exist, reside in either heaven or hell during Life In Between.

For the sake of full disclosure, a very interesting story unfolds in 1 Samuel 28 that speaks, at least in part, to this question of ghosts. As it begins, King Saul has been rejected by God as the anointed king over Israel because of his persistent disobedience. When this happened, the Spirit of God departed from him. The prophet Samuel delivered this message to Saul personally, confirming his departure from God's plan for Israel (1 Samuel 15:26–28).

In 1 Samuel 28, Saul was facing a battle with the Philistines and wanted to hear from the Lord as he used to. But no longer able to hear directly from the Lord, he approached a medium, or spiritist, in a place called Endor and asked the witch to call on the spirit of Samuel, who had since passed away, so he could consult with him. Reluctantly, the woman agreed to call up Samuel's departed spirit and, to my surprise as I studied the Bible to answer this question, the spirit of Samuel appeared.

The king asked the medium what she saw—he apparently couldn't see Samuel's spirit—and she replied, "I see a *ghostly* figure coming up out of the earth" (v. 13, emphasis added). Then Saul asked her what he looked like, and she said, "An old man wearing a robe is coming up" (v. 14).

Samuel's first words to Saul were, "Why have you disturbed me by bringing me up?" (v. 15). It is clear that Samuel didn't inhabit the earth but was called up from his resting place. Based on Jesus' teaching, we will assume this is Abraham's side (Luke 16:19–31). Saul and Samuel then proceeded to have a conversation in which Samuel essentially recounted all the bad news he had already given Saul the last time they were together, about the Lord's anointing being removed because of his disobedience. The conversation then came to an end.

Based on this story, it appears the work of mediums can, at times, be real. However, over and over again the Bible warns us to stay completely away from this activity of calling up departed spirits.

Do not turn to mediums or seek out spiritists, for you will be defiled by them. I am the LORD your God.

—LEVITICUS 19:31

The prophet Isaiah gives us the same warning with a great piece of advice:

When someone tells you to consult mediums and spiritists, who whisper and mutter, should not a people inquire of their God? Why consult the dead on behalf of the living?

—ISAIAH 8:19

The practice of mediums can be very real, and that is very scary to me. My strong recommendation to you is to stay away from it at all costs. It's clear that God's plan for the spirits of the dead in Life In Between is that they remain in the places set aside for them during this time, not to be called up as Samuel was. If we need information, if we need truth, if we need direction, we are admonished to consult God. If we do that, we will never be led astray.

Are our loved ones in heaven watching over us?

It would be comforting to me if I knew my mother was watching over me from heaven. I am not so sure it would be as comforting for her, given the ongoing unrest in our world. Maybe she *is* watching over me, but as I dig through the pages of Scripture I can find no evidence that folks who have died in the body and whose spirits are with the Lord have been given the same assignments as angels to be ministering spirits.

If you think about it, there are no tears in heaven or anguish or grief, worry or fear. Would that be possible if our loved ones looked down on us and saw the bad things that happen in this world because of sin? Would they be able to see their loved ones go through hurting or harm and not worry? At the same time, if their spirits wondered about or were restless about something, it would be like God to give them just what they needed to know to keep them in a state of peace and rest. Rest assured that while the Bible doesn't say anything explicit, we must trust that God will make sure our loved ones are comforted and give them just what they need to have perfect peace.

With that said, remember the following truths:

- God is watching over you, day and night. (Psalm 139:1–4)
- Our loved ones are in a better place. (Philippians 1:23)
- We will see them again and spend eternity with them. (1 Thessalonians 5:10–11)
- God gives those of us who trust him everything we need in Life Now, so we don't need to disturb our loved ones who have preceded us. (Philippians 4:19)

Is there such a thing as purgatory or Limbo?

This is a concept taught primarily by the Roman Catholic Church and the Greek Orthodox Church. Today, when someone says he is in "limbo," he means that he is stuck between where he is and where he wants to be. This is the idea behind the Catholic notion of Limbo or purgatory, an additional place in Life In Between, really a state of existence. There, it is taught, people who are already saved and at peace with the Church go to pay penance or express sorrow over their sins for the purpose of purifying and perfecting themselves to be in God's presence. The length of stay in purgatory can last for a few hours under mild circumstances or for thousands of years in "hell-like" conditions.

Catholic leaders don't see this place as punishment from God but as an act of God's mercy. They suggest that without it, it would be impossible for most believers in Christ ever to go to heaven in God's actual presence. Even though Christ has forgiven all sins, believers must approach God on a continual basis to receive that forgiveness. This is why Catholics go to "confession" each week.

As I studied this concept from Catholic sources, I noted that they all cited quotes from the pope, from catechisms, and from church councils as the authority for this doctrine. There is one primary passage out of a book called 2 Maccabees that is often cited as scriptural support for this view. If you're not familiar with 2 Maccabees, it, along with fifteen other books, make up what are called the Apocryphal books. Catholics embrace some of these books as Scripture, while most Protestant denominations do not.[4]

In 2 Maccabees 12 a noble man named Judas gathers the bodies of a few fallen Jewish soldiers to bury them. He finds them wearing jewelry from an idol, which was forbidden and is therefore a sin. Because the men died before they could confess this sin and offer penance, Judas has the men offer prayers for the dead that this sin might be "blotted out." In addition, they take up a cash collection and send it to Jerusalem as a sin offering on behalf of the dead men. Verse 45 states, "Therefore he made atonement for the dead, that they might be delivered from their sin" (NRSVA).

Catholics believe the spirits of Christians who die with sins not addressed do not go directly into the presence of God but rather go to a place or state of purgatory—basically an in-between place for believers, similar to Abraham's side, where they are given the chance to make up for the sins they did not confess during Life Now. Once sufficient penance has been offered, the believer is taken into the presence of God to join up with the other saints. "Gifts or services rendered to the church, prayers by the priests, and Masses provided by relatives or friends on behalf of the deceased can shorten, alleviate, or eliminate the sojourn of the soul in purgatory."[5] Basically, believers who are alive can pray and invite a priest to pray on their behalf to shorten their loved one's stay in purgatory.

What do I think about this? When a Christian belief is developed, we look for more than one isolated scripture on which to build the doctrine. Even if I embraced 2 Maccabees as Scripture, it would be difficult to create an iron-clad concept of purgatory around this single passage. As I understand it, Catholics hold the official words of the pope, accepted creeds and catechisms written by the Church, and official Church councils on a par with Scripture. If you embrace this idea, there is plenty of authoritative teaching to support the concept of purgatory.

As for me, while I have great respect for the thoughts and teachings of the pope and the Catholic Church on a number of issues, I do not put their teachings on the same authoritative level as the Bible. Therefore, I don't find enough evidence to suggest there is such a place as purgatory or a need for such a place. I think this viewpoint underestimates all that Christ's work on the cross did for us:

He has reconciled you by Christ's physical body through death to present you holy in his sight, without blemish and free from accusation.

—COLOSSIANS 1:22

When Christians' physical bodies die, our spirits are *presented* to the presence of Christ *without blemish and free from accusation.* I certainly deserve hell—and even purgatory, if it existed—but thanks to the grace of God, the righteousness of Christ is charged to my account (Romans 5:12–21).

Are there different degrees of hell?

My first exposure to Dante Alighieri's fourteenth-century poem the *Divine Comedy* was in college. This epic allegory records Dante's journey through hell, guided by the ancient Roman poet Virgil. Dante's vision of hell includes nine concentric circles of suffering located in the center of Earth. Within the circle are twenty-four subdivisions. Pretty complex imagination.

Each ring represents a different degree of evil in which the resident engaged while on this earth, with a corresponding punishment to match. Fortune-tellers, for example, reside in one circle.

For eternity they must walk forward with their heads on backward, unable to see what is ahead, because they tried to see the future through forbidden means.

These are the circles in Dante's construct of hell:

Circle 1: *Limbo*

Circle 2: *Lust*

Circle 3: *Gluttony*

Circle 4: *Greed*

Circe 5: *Wrath*

Circle 6: *Heresy*

Circle 7: *Violence*

Circle 8: *Fraud*

Circle 9: *Treachery*

According to Dante, Satan himself resides at the end of this journey, where the greatest amount of punishment is executed.

Truthfully, I find all this to be fascinating and disturbing at the same time. This is the kind of stuff I don't like to read or think about right before I go to sleep, lest the content show up in my crazy dreams and wake me up in a cold sweat. But the question remains, what does the Bible say?

Looking through every conceivable passage, I can find no explicit content regarding the different degrees of hell—whether we're talking about Hades or the lake of fire. With that said, if we come to the end and discover there are, in fact, degrees of punishment, we shouldn't be surprised. Let me lay out my reasoning from scriptures that touch on this subject.

- *God is just.* He executes punishment based on the sin committed (Exodus 21:23–25; Deuteronomy 25:2–3). This is how God executed justice under the law of Moses. It is reasonable he would do the same in the final courtroom at the Great White Throne judgment (Revelation 20:11–15).

  Since believers are rewarded on the basis of their works on earth, it stands to reason that unbelievers are punished on the basis of their works (1 Corinthians 3:8, 11–15; 2 Corinthians 5:10; Colossians 3:23–25).

- *The Bible teaches there is such a thing as a "greater sin."* Jesus told Pontius Pilate at his trial: "You would have no power over me if it were not given to you from above. Therefore the one who handed me over to you is guilty of a greater sin" (John 19:11). Jesus was referring to the Jewish leaders. What they had done to him, Jesus said, was a greater sin than what Pilate would do.

- *The Bible teaches that people who have received more revelation and reject it will be punished more severely than the ones who knew less* (Luke 12:42–48; 2 Peter 2:20–21). The writer of Hebrews reinforced this teaching of Jesus:

  > Anyone who rejected the law of Moses died without mercy on the testimony of two or three witnesses. How much more severely do you think someone deserves to be punished who has trampled the Son of God underfoot, who has treated as an unholy thing the blood of the covenant that sanctified them, and who has insulted the Spirit of grace? (Hebrews 10:28–29)

With all these scriptures laid side by side, it seems reasonable that there are degrees of punishment in hell. Yet, the Bible doesn't spell it out explicitly, so we must not hold the idea dogmatically but loosely. Here is what I know for sure: *regardless of degrees of punishment, hell is a place to be avoided at all cost. The good news is, Jesus paid all the cost.* Accept his payment, and never experience the place at all.

Can we earn wings?

In the ever-so-charming 1946 movie *It's a Wonderful Life*, in an effort to finally earn his wings, the angel Clarence comes down to help George Bailey.[6]

Where did the idea of human spirits in heaven having or earning wings come from?

In the Bible, angelic beings called *cherubim* and *seraphim* are referred to as having wings. In Isaiah 6 the prophet enters the temple and sees "the Lord, high and exalted, seated on a throne; and the train of his robe filled the temple" (v. 1). Isaiah then goes on to tell us he saw these supernatural beings called seraphim, each having six wings. But nowhere in Scripture do we see human spirits having the same.

Clarence was a man who had died and later referred to himself as an angel (specifically, an AS2—Angel Second Class). This is cute in the movie, but it is not true in real life. In the Bible, humans and angels are two totally different beings with two totally different story lines. Some angels have wings, and that is amazing to us; we humans have experienced salvation, and that is amazing to angels (1 Peter 1:10–12). So, sorry, Clarence, no wings.

LIFE FOREVER

CHAPTER FOUR

What Happens If I Don't Know Christ When He Returns?

RON WILLIAMSON'S LIFE STARTED WITH PROMISE. Born in Oklahoma in 1953, he was the youngest of three siblings and the only son. It didn't take long for folks to realize that Ron was a gifted athlete. While he excelled in all sports, baseball was his passion. During his senior year of high school, in 1971, he was the second-round draft pick by the Oakland Athletics to play in their minor league club. Shoulder injuries derailed his pursuit a few years in, but he got a second chance in 1976 with the New York Yankees farm club as a pitcher. Because he was unable to restore the health and strength of his shoulder, his aspirations of major league greatness came to an end the next year.

Ron, no doubt discouraged, moved back to Oklahoma to live with his mother. Soon addiction to drugs and alcohol replaced his passion for baseball. Depression and mental illness reared their ugly heads to escalate his journey into despair.

63

In 1988 Ron Williamson was convicted for the rape and murder of Debbie Carter and received the death penalty for his crimes. The judge said with the raspy voice of an umpire, "You're out!"

Every day for the next eleven years, Ron lived with the horror and anticipation of execution. He was benched, waiting not to get back out on the field, but to die.[1]

For the person who has died without coming to know Christ as his or her personal Savior, waiting for the return of Christ is like sitting on death row. You have already been sentenced to death for the choice you made in life, and now you are imprisoned as you await a more final death. Not exactly the pick-me-up message we like hearing from Christian authors, but it is true and needs to be told. This is, without question, the hardest chapter I have ever written. I don't pen these words flippantly or casually but with great care.

Let's turn to the Scriptures to see how the events will unfold.

In the book of Revelation, God gave the apostle John a vivid vision of what is yet to come. It is as though John sat in an IMAX theater with 3-D glasses wrapped around his face.

Everything started moving toward a conclusion, the end of life as we know it on this earth. Here is John's vivid description of the day Christ returns to earth as warrior and conqueror.

> I saw heaven standing open and there before me was a white horse, whose rider is called Faithful and True. With justice he judges and wages war. His eyes are like blazing fire, and on his head are many crowns. He has a name written on him that no one knows but he himself. He is dressed in a robe dipped in blood, and his name is the Word of God. The armies of heaven were

following him, riding on white horses and dressed in fine linen, white and clean. Coming out of his mouth is a sharp sword with which to strike down the nations. "He will rule them with an iron scepter." He treads the winepress of the fury of the wrath of God Almighty. On his robe and on his thigh he has this name written:

KING OF KINGS AND LORD OF LORDS.

—REVELATION 19:11–16

In this battle Jesus apprehends the two main cohorts of Satan: the Beast and the False Prophet. The next character to be captured is the archenemy of God, Satan himself (the "ancient serpent," Revelation 12:9; 20:2). There are several views on the timeline for this event, but it is not pertinent for our purposes.[2] At the end of the day, Jesus defeats all his enemies, Satan included!

Then we see the final judgment of humans—either alive at the time of Christ's return or already imprisoned in Hades—who rejected Christ's offer of forgiveness and God's vision for the new kingdom. Let's take a closer look at the passage together.

THE GREAT WHITE THRONE—JESUS JUDGES THE WORKS OF UNBELIEVERS

Then I saw a great white throne and him who was seated on it. The earth and the heavens fled from his presence, and there was no place for them.

—REVELATION 20:11

At Jesus' first coming he came as a vulnerable baby lying in a manger. At his second, he will come as a warrior and a judge. All the wrong deeds we thought had slipped past God's notice and all the evil done in dark places will be brought out into the open, and all will be given a verdict and punishment.

This is such a big deal, such a grand event, that "the earth and the heavens [flee] from his presence." I have no mental model for this cataclysmic event. Essentially, the earth and our atmosphere will have served their purpose and will come to an end. Are you a bit intimidated, as I am? Good! I think this is what God is going for.

Let's keep reading:

And I saw the dead, great and small, standing before the throne, and books were opened. Another book was opened, which is the book of life. The dead were judged according to what they had done as recorded in the books. The sea gave up the dead that were in it, and death and Hades gave up the dead that were in them, and each person was judged according to what they had done.

—REVELATION 20:12–13

Do you remember the rich man waiting in Hades (Luke 16)? Now is his time. John tells us that all the spirits who have been in the holding tank of Hades, away from God's presence in the intermediate state, will receive resurrected bodies of some sort and will then stand before Jesus to be officially and fairly judged. Thank goodness, this judgment is not for believers. Jesus clearly said:

Very truly I tell you, whoever hears my word and believes him who sent me has eternal life and will not be judged but has crossed over from death to life.

—JOHN 5:24

Paul affirmed Jesus' teaching in his letter to the Romans:

Therefore, there is now no condemnation for those who are in Christ Jesus. . . . Who will bring any charge against those whom God has chosen? It is God who justifies. Who then is the one who condemns? No one.

—ROMANS 8:1, 33–34

Jesus took our day in court two thousand years ago. When Jesus stood on trial before Pontius Pilate and was condemned to die, all the guilt of those who now believe was nailed to the cross and paid for once and for all (Romans 3:21–26). If you are a believer in Jesus, take a moment and let this truth sink into your soul.

Now, how will unbelievers be judged? The books will be opened.

THE BOOKS—CONTAINING DETAILED RECORDS OF EVERYTHING EACH PERSON DID ON EARTH

The book of Revelation mentions two sets of books. The first contains a detailed log of everything each person has ever done—the good and the bad. Not a single action escapes Jesus' notice. Sort of a divine iCloud storage file, if you will. When the time for judgment comes, the records will be submitted as evidence to convict the defendant.

This is not going to be about good deeds outweighing bad deeds, or vice versa, as so many seem to think. After thirty years of being a pastor, I am still amazed by the number of people who believe God is going to grade on a curve. They know they have done wrong, have been downright mean-spirited, and have mistreated others, particularly those closest to them. Yet when they watch the nightly news and see terrorists or child abductors, they conclude, *I'm not as bad as those folks. I am a good person. I haven't killed anybody. I pay most of my taxes. I volunteer from time to time at the local homeless shelter. I'm not perfect, but I try my best to be good. I don't expect to win the Mother Teresa award, but overall I think I will receive a passing grade.*

Funerals may have helped create this mind-set. I have yet to conduct a funeral or sit in a memorial service where it is proclaimed that the deceased had refused to receive Christ and is therefore now in hell. In an attempt to comfort the family, pastors may say what they want to hear—that their relative is in the arms of Jesus. The person attending the service ponders those words and then often concludes, *If that ole cuss could get in, with how he lived* his *life, then I am definitely a shoo-in.*

Twenty years ago I made a commitment not to confuse people this way anymore. If I am unsure of where the person stood with Christ, I simply say, "If Bill were standing here today, based on what he now knows about the afterlife, this is what he would want you to know." I then share the gospel from the Scriptures, making the basis for salvation and the decision as clear and as plain as I can. It is sensitive to the family and also doesn't misguide the audience.

The Bible tells us that just one bad deed makes us guilty and exposes our sin nature, making us unfit for God's eternal community (James 2:10). Anyone who claims he has committed only one bad deed has now committed at least two—the one he admitted to and the lie he just told! In any event, everyone facing judgment before the Great White Throne is guilty. There is no potential claim of "reasonable doubt." The evidence is conclusive.

Then the judicial assistants will consult the other book opened before the divine court. It is the Book of Life, containing the names of all the people who accepted Christ's pardon in Life Now. If an individual's name is not included in this important book, all the books will be closed, the gavel of Judge Jesus will descend with one final thud, and court will adjourn.

What happens next is awful, but it is the only thing a righteous, just, and loving God can do:[3]

> Anyone whose name [is] not found written in the book of life [will be] thrown into the lake of fire.
>
> —REVELATION 20:14–15

THE LAKE OF FIRE—THE FINAL DESTINATION OF SATAN, DEMONS, DEATH, HADES, AND UNBELIEVERS

Apart from a brief figurative reference in the book of James, Jesus is the only one who refers to this place by name—*Gehenna* in the Greek. Maybe this is because Jesus not only saw it but created it for this very purpose. In Revelation, God gave John a vision of this burning lake of sulfur for us to see for ourselves.

This is the place in the horror movie where many drop their heads and put their hands over their eyes to prevent seeing what happens next. But we must look.

We learn in Revelation 20:10 that Satan is cast into Gehenna first. That is appropriate in my estimation. No one objects.

Next, death and Hades are thrown into the lake of fire (v. 14). Essentially, this is the end of death as we know it. Death dies. I can't wait to be there and experience this event because of all that death has taken away from me and all the fear it has created in me. From this point on, death will be no more.

Then Hades, the holding tank for unbelieving spirits awaiting judgment, will no longer be needed, so it will also be cast into the smoldering lake. Life In Between will have come to an end. All we are now left with is eternity, or Life Forever.

The final group to be cast into the lake of fire consists of all those who rejected God's vision for eternal life with him. They will have been judged fairly according to what they have done and will have been given their final verdict, painful as it is for Jesus to do so (2 Peter 3:9).

What happens to them once their bodies enter the lake? There are two views on this: eternal punishing and eternal punishment.

Eternal Punishing

Currently, eternal punishing is the most widely accepted view. It has been, without doubt, the dominant belief throughout the twentieth century. Eternal punishing points to the convicted unbeliever being forever conscious and alive to experience eternal agony for rejecting the vision of God. This is not just banishment from participation in God's kingdom but an ongoing tormenting.

While some believe that Hades is the intermediate holding tank, not a place of actual fire, they think *this* place, the lake of fire, *is* an actual place of fire. Revelation 20:10 tells us that, at least for Satan and his team, "they will be tormented day and night for ever and ever."

Therefore, the assumption is made that this will be the fate of nonbelievers as well. How dreadfully frightening.

Eternal Punishment

There is a second view gaining some ground among modern Christians, but it is not a new idea. It was held by some ancient church fathers, such as Ignatius of Antioch, Irenaeus of Lyons, Arnobius of Sicca, and Athanasius the Great.[4] This view is commonly called *annihilation* or *conditional immortality*.[5] It lost steam with the rise of the teaching of Augustine of Hippo, who held to the previous position, but is now coming back up.

Annihilation suggests that when the body enters the lake, both the body and soul cease to exist. They die once and for all. Jesus warned: "Do not be afraid of those who kill the body but cannot kill the soul. Rather, be afraid of the One who can destroy both soul and body in hell" (Matthew 10:28). This point of view suggests Jesus can not only do this, but he will do it in the end for those who have rejected his offer.

John called this "the second death" (Revelation 21:18), the first death being of the perishable body we received from Adam.

71

One might ask, "How many times do we die before we actually die?"

This interpretation says, "This is it; dead is dead."

Dr. Roger Olson, in his research on theological views that qualify as acceptable positions to hold within orthodox Christianity, suggests this is one of them.[6] In my own theological training, I was taught this view bordered on heresy. Today many theologians may still not lean toward this view, but it is no longer considered heretical to do so.

Frankly, I don't know which view is correct. I can tell you eternal punishment is the one I want to be the right answer. I have family and friends who absolutely did not call on the name of Jesus in Life Now who will be in this line. For whatever reason, they rejected God's offer. They didn't want to be a part of God's eternal kingdom, and now he will simply honor their choice. I can accept that as completely loving and just. But it is hard to imagine this agonizing punishment going on for eternity for people I love so much.

Some people oppose this view because they think it might encourage folks to reject God if they know there is ultimately an out or an end to the punishment if God happens to turn out to be real. We must be reminded, though, that God is not saving us *from* hell but saving us *for* eternal life with him.

WE CAN'T DEVELOP OUR THEOLOGY BASED ON HOW PEOPLE MIGHT OR MIGHT NOT RESPOND TO IT.

Someone who receives Christ's offer of forgiveness simply to avoid eternal punishment doesn't really understand, nor will they get, the offer God is making. God wants people to choose him and life with him forever. We can't develop our theology based on how people might or might not respond to it.

Both options, in my opinion, are possible. For sure, there is a day coming when the truth will be revealed. Bottom line: neither option sounds desirable to me, but I sure hope it is "eternal punishment" versus "eternal punishing." How about you?

DIVINE EXONERATION

After eleven years on death row, something unexpected happened for Ron Williamson. DNA testing revealed he was not Debbie Carter's rapist or killer after all. It was a man named Glen Gore who was guilty. Ron was released from prison.

Can you imagine the first morning he woke up as a free man and realized he wasn't on death row anymore? No more nightmares of the day he would be injected with a substance that would take his life. No more counting down the days in fear as the ultimate day of punishment approached. It was over!

What a beautiful turn of events for Williamson. It's the same for those who accept Christ's offer.

There is good news for those of us who are still breathing. We are still in Life Now and have the opportunity to change our eternal destinies. Jesus was on death row for thirty-three years. From the foundation of the world, it was determined that he would be slain.

We have already committed the crimes. We are guilty. But God offers you and me the deal of a lifetime. If we accept Christ's offer in Life Now, before we die, all our crimes and wrongs will be transferred over to Jesus. The record books in heaven will be the proof.

When the books are opened, no sins will be listed next to our names. The record will show that Jesus himself was convicted and executed for these crimes.

Ron Williamson was exonerated because he was innocent. We will be exonerated, not because we are innocent, but because Christ already paid for our crimes.

Keep in mind, this offer is only good if you act on it before you die. Once this body dies, the deal is off. But if you do accept it now, by faith, you will never sit on death row in Hades, and you will not be executed. Instead, you will live forever in the presence of God, which will be the greatest gift of all. It's much more than a Get Out of Jail Free card; it's a key to a future beyond our wildest imaginations. Come with me as we finally dive into my favorite part of this whole journey.

CHAPTER FIVE

What Happens If I Do Know Christ When He Returns?

I HAVE AMAZING MEMORIES OF GROWING UP IN MY mom's care. She came from a poor family in southwestern Pennsylvania. She married my dad at eighteen, and when I was three they moved to Cleveland, Ohio, where my dad secured a job with Caterpillar assembling forklifts.

During my growing-up years, my mother loved and sacrificed so much for my three siblings and me. She spent all her money and time on us; I can barely remember her doing anything just for herself. So, several years ago, when I was finally at a place in my life with a little financial margin, I called my mother to tell her my wife and I were taking her and my dad on an all-expense-paid trip to the magnificent Niagara Falls, about a two-and-a-half-hour drive from Cleveland.

We had reserved rooms in a turn-of-the-century, opulent hotel on the Canadian side of the border, facing the falls. She was going

75

to be so embarrassed and uncomfortable, believing she didn't belong in a place like this and that it was just too extravagant. This was exactly the reaction I wanted.

But when I made the call to Mom a few months out to tell her what I had planned, she told me she wasn't feeling well. Initially, I thought she was just trying to wiggle out of the trip. However, as the next few months unfolded and her illness got worse, I really started to worry. That's when I decided to fly back to my parents' home ahead of my family—as you already know from the opening chapter—three days before our previously scheduled arrival.

Three days later my mother died of advanced pancreatic cancer. We canceled the trip just two days before we were to take off. I was finally in a place to do something special for my mother for all she had given me as her child, and I missed it forever by two days!

I was devastated on a number of levels. Something changed in me that day. Maybe it wasn't a change but an awakening of something that had been there all along. I slipped into a crisis—a place of despair. I suddenly realized I didn't have a vision for the afterlife in Christ that was truly compelling to me. In some ways I doubted if anything really would happen after we died. This is a pretty awkward place to find yourself when you are the pastor of a large church. People sort of expect you to believe in heaven. But what I have discovered in the course of my journey is that a confession of belief from the heart is often preceded with a confession of unbelief from the lips.

The thing I miss most about being with my mom is the comfort she always gave me. Whenever I was sad or hurting, all I had to do was lay my head in the crevice between her head and her shoulders. It was the safest, sweetest place on earth.

The last two days of my mom's life, when no one else was in the room, I would crawl into the bed with her and tuck my head in that warm spot of intense love while tears rolled down my face. I'd thought I would have more time. Now I was trying to soak in a lifetime in just two days, unsure we would ever see each other again.

After she was gone, I turned all my attention over the next few years to getting my questions sorted out. What did the Bible really say about "what's next"? I was all ears for a fresh vision not watered down by the syrupy chatter at funerals.

A VISION FOR WHAT'S NEXT

Paul quoted Isaiah in his first letter to the Corinthians:

> "What no eye has seen,
> what no ear has heard,
> and what no human mind has conceived"—
> the things God has prepared for those who love him.
>
> —1 CORINTHIANS 2:9

During my years of sitting in pews I heard many pastors and singers introduce songs by quoting this verse and saying, "Folks, we just have no idea what God has in store for us." But for some reason they would never read the next verse, which went on to say, "These are the things God has revealed to us by his Spirit" (v. 10).

The full vision of the afterlife may have been concealed to the people of the Old Testament, but now, through Christ and with the illumination of the Holy Spirit, the New Testament Scriptures reveal a vivid vision of what is to come "for those who love him." God has told us what happens next.

But before we dive in more fully to this vision, let's review what we've discovered together about our spirits' journeys through the stages of life up to this point.

When we die and Life Now comes to an end, our spirits go to be with the Lord, leaving behind our physical bodies to be buried or cremated (we'll talk more about this a bit later). We don't know much about Life In Between, the intermediate state, but we do know that it is a good thing for the believer in Jesus. In this stage, we are waiting for the ultimate promise of Jesus that will be initiated when he returns to earth. It is my opinion those in heaven with God right now are living outside of space and time. There is no real sense of time elapsing, which means life is not droning on day after day while naked spirits wait for Christ to make his move. People in heaven are really in a state of being, not so much a place of time. I'll let you ponder this on your own for a bit.

When Christ does make his move and returns again to earth, though, we step into Life Forever, the final stage, which catalyzes a number of amazing transformations. Revelation 21–22, the last two chapters of the Bible, give us a pretty clear vision of what is to come in those days. Let me just give you the bottom line, the four things I discovered during my search for the truth that excite me to no end about what's next.

Discovery #1: We are going to receive new bodies.

This is a very big deal. It is what the New Testament writers got excited about almost every time the subject of the afterlife was brought up. The ultimate hope for the believer is not found in dying and going up to heaven as a spirit being, but about receiving a resurrected body, just as Jesus did.

Roger Olson makes this poignant observation:

> It would be impossible to discover any single point of greater agreement in the history of Christian thought than this single one: *the future bodily resurrection of the dead is the blessed hope of all who are in Christ Jesus by faith.* Over two millennia the church's leaders and faithful theologians have unanimously taught this above the immortality of souls and as more important than some ethereal intermediate state between bodily death and bodily resurrection when Christ returns. And yet, . . . it seems that the vast majority of Christians do not know this and neglect belief in bodily resurrection in favor of belief in immediate postmortem heavenly, spiritual existence as ghost-like beings (or even angels!) "forever with the Lord in heaven."[1]

The entire chapter of 1 Corinthians 15 lays it all out in detail. Listen to these words:

> But Christ has indeed been raised from the dead, the firstfruits of those who have fallen asleep. For since death came through a man, the resurrection of the dead comes also through a man. For as in Adam all die, so in Christ all will be made alive. . . . I declare to you, brothers and sisters, that flesh and blood cannot inherit the

kingdom of God, nor does the perishable inherit the imperishable. Listen, I tell you a mystery: We will not all sleep, but we will all be changed—in a flash, in the twinkling of an eye, at the last trumpet. For the trumpet will sound, the dead will be raised imperishable, and we will be changed. For the perishable must clothe itself with the imperishable, and the mortal with immortality. When the perishable has been clothed with the imperishable, and the mortal with immortality, then the saying that is written will come true: "Death has been swallowed up in victory."

—I CORINTHIANS 15:20–22, 50–54

The body each of us currently has is from the first Adam. It is perishable and must die. And, boy, does it. When Christ walked the earth he had a body from the first Adam that was obviously perishable; otherwise, he would not have died on the cross. When he was raised from the dead after three days, he received a resurrected body that is imperishable. This is the hope of the believer in Jesus.

But look again at Paul's words. This transaction doesn't take place when the first body dies but "at the last trumpet." This refers to Jesus coming for the second time to claim his own. At that moment the dead will be raised with their imperishable bodies, and for those of us who are still living, our earthly bodies will be changed into immortal ones.

Discovery #2: The final destination for believers is not up there but down here.

God is going to do what he did in Genesis 1–2 all over again. That's why the theme of the first two chapters of the Bible is so similar to that of the last two chapters of the Bible. God is going to create a *new heaven and a new earth* (Revelation 21:1). Human history is not really a straight line but a circle that winds us all the way around to where we started—the original vision of God.

When all that we consider to be the end times comes to a close, we will live on the new earth—a real place. I have a mental model for this. As I am writing this chapter, I am on a cruise ship sailing from Belize back to Houston. The sun is up. The water is blue. The breeze is gentle. The day before I was with my wife, son, and daughter-in-law in a magnificent rain forest on the island of Roátan, Honduras, and we are now heading home to the beautiful hill country north of San Antonio, Texas, where God did some of his finest work. I love earth living. And the astonishing thing is that the new earth is going to be even more amazing than the current one. God did it once; I believe he can and will do it again. Remove all the bad stuff, and I am ready to make the shift right now.

If I were only a spirit being, and an angel were to describe earth to me as a big round ball that is suspended in midair and rotates around a big ball of fire, along with a collection of other giant balls of matter, I would have a hard time believing something so spectacular could be created from nothing. If I were told of the amazing intricacies that exist on earth and in the heavens to create such order and balance, it would just seem too far-fetched. But I have seen it with my own two eyes and have experienced its grandeur for more than half a century. Not only do I believe God can do it again, but I get pretty excited about it!

I am careful not to call this final state heaven. When most people I talk to think of the word *heaven*, they think of a place up in the sky or atmosphere where we will spend all eternity. Appropriately, the place where our spirits hang out in Life In Between in the presence of God while we await the return of Christ and our resurrected bodies is called "heaven," but remember that what is to come in Life Forever is different and separate from that intermediate space. To keep this vision of God distinct and fresh, I like to refer to it as the new earth or the new kingdom. Maybe think of it this way: when we die, we go up to heaven; when Christ returns, he brings heaven to a brand-new earth.

Discovery #3: God is not staying up there, but he is coming down here . . .

. . . to be with us as he was with Adam and Eve, to take walks with us in the cool of the day (Genesis 3:8). Revelation 21:3 tells us, "And I heard a loud voice from the throne saying, 'Look! God's dwelling place is now among the people, and he will dwell with them. They will be his people, and God himself will be with them and be their God.'"

I feel the presence of God in my life now; I really do. I pray almost nonstop. I sense he is with me and in me, because he is (Matthew 28:20; John 14:16). However, having God actually here with us where we can see him is a dramatic improvement, if you ask me. It points to the ultimate restoration of the relationship that Adam and Eve rejected so long ago.

Truthfully, I can't imagine meeting Jesus face-to-face. I have been to Israel and walked on the ground where he walked. I took a boat ride on the Sea of Galilee, where he calmed the waves and miraculously walked on water during the storm (Matthew 14:22–34;

Mark 6:45–53). That is the closest I have come to knowing what it must have been like to live during the same time Jesus walked here on earth. But in the coming days, when all has been made new again, I will get to meet him, shake his hand, hug his neck, share a meal with him, and hear him teach live.

Then I ponder meeting the Father and the Holy Spirit. Do they possess physical bodies, as Jesus does? Will I be able to touch them and feel their breath on my face as I talk with them? My heart is pounding right now as I realize that all the images I have had of the Father will be altered to reality. I think we are in for a big surprise; I am just not sure what it will look like. To come face-to-face with Pure Love, now, that is going to be something.

Discovery #4: God will form a grand new city beyond our imaginations where we will live with him on the new earth.

Let's take in the description of God's new city from John's vision (read slowly):

Then I saw "a new heaven and a new earth," for the first heaven and the first earth had passed away, and there was no longer any sea. I saw the Holy City, the new Jerusalem, coming down out of heaven from God, prepared as a bride beautifully dressed for her husband. And I heard a loud voice from the throne saying, "Look! God's dwelling place is now among the people, and he will dwell with them. They will be his people, and God himself will be with them and be their God. 'He will wipe every tear from their eyes. There will be no more death' or mourning or crying or pain, for the old order of things has passed away."

He who was seated on the throne said, "I am making everything new!"

—Revelation 21:1–5

Is this not just incredible? "The old order of things has passed away." I think of all the times—after they have experienced an unavoidable disappointment or tragedy—I have said to my children or people I pastor, "That's just life." Won't need to use that cliché again in God's new city; tragedy and disappointment do not have a residence on the new earth. In the old order of things, families broke up and crushed the spirits of adults and altered the trust quota of children. That's not how things will turn out in the new order under Christ.

Eighty-eight percent of people today burn through a lot of anxiety worrying about health-related things that will never come to fruition,[2] but there will be no need to do that anymore in the days to come. Bad things can't happen in our new digs. The fear that overtakes a person who is given a frightening diagnosis—his body is overcome with cancer, she is experiencing the onset of Alzheimer's, or a son or daughter is in the first stage of ALS—will no longer be a factor. No more will such rude news flashes ever happen again in the new way of life. The uncontrollable tears that roll down the face of a child, spouse, or friend who watches a person he or she loved so dearly breathe that last breath will be wiped away. No more wondering how we are going to do life without that person.

I don't know about you, but I am ready to have every tear wiped from my eyes by the index finger of Jesus himself.

Now keep reading slowly for a fuller description of the new city. Let's start with the size of the city.

> The angel who talked with me had a measuring rod of gold to measure the city, its gates and its walls. The city was laid out like a square, as long as it was wide. He measured the city with the rod and found it to be 12,000 stadia in length, and as wide and high as it is long. The angel measured the wall using human measurement, and it was 144 cubits thick.
>
> —REVELATION 21:15–17

Let me put this in some concrete terms. The city is essentially a fifteen-hundred-mile symmetrical cube. For some context, fifteen hundred miles is about the distance between the southernmost tip of Florida and Maine. If my measurements are correct, the wall around the city will be about seventy yards thick. This is a whole new vision for living. Scenes out of sci-fi movies come to mind, where people are living on multiple layers and traveling in hovercraft. I grew up watching a cartoon called *The Jetsons*, and this is how they lived, in a vast, sprawling city raised high above the ground.[3] Who ever would have thought that this might be our best vision of the afterlife?

How many people might be able to live in such a city? Well, someone did the math, as we see in Ron Rhodes's *The Wonder of Heaven*:

> Someone calculated that if this structure is cube-shaped, it would allow for 20 billion residents, each having his or her own private 75-acre cube. If each residence were smaller, then there

is room to accommodate 100 thousand billion people. Even then, plenty of room is left over for parks, streets and other things you would see in any normal city.[4]

And this is just the main city. There is still the rest of the earth for us to explore that will be grander and more pristine than it is right now. It's already pretty amazing right now, so the idea of it getting better blows my mind.

What about the mansions people talk about? Jesus told his disciples that he was going ahead of them to prepare a place for them.

Do not let your hearts be troubled. You believe in God; believe also in me. My Father's house has many rooms; if that were not so, would I have told you that I am going there to prepare a place for you? And if I go and prepare a place for you, I will come back and take you to be with me that you also may be where I am.

—JOHN 14:1–3

This is what he was talking about. When your name is found in the Book of Life, construction plans are laid out for your personal dwelling. What kind of place is God constructing for you and me? The King James Version calls them "mansions." The New International Version calls them "rooms," which seems to be somewhat of a downgrade. Which is correct?

The Old Latin translation of the Bible translated this Greek word that Jesus used as "mansions."[5] The King James translators followed suit. However, the Greek word is more literally translated as "dwelling places," so sadly, the word *rooms* is more accurate. But

"My Father's house has many rooms" indicates that we will each have a room within God's house, versus a separate, stand-alone house for every believer. Proximity to the Father is far better, in my opinion, than my own separate pad. It may or may not be an actual mansion, but regardless, we can trust that God's provision will be more than enough. Remember: Jesus is not only the God of the universe; he is also a pretty good carpenter (Mark 6:3).

John went on to describe the aesthetics of the city in a bit more detail:

> The wall was made of jasper, and the city of pure gold, as pure as glass. The foundations of the city walls were decorated with every kind of precious stone. The first foundation was jasper, the second sapphire, the third agate, the fourth emerald, the fifth onyx, the sixth ruby, the seventh chrysolite, the eighth beryl, the ninth topaz, the tenth turquoise, the eleventh jacinth, and the twelfth amethyst. The twelve gates were twelve pearls, each gate made of a single pearl. The great street of the city was of gold, as pure as transparent glass.
>
> —REVELATION 21:18–21

Here are the pearly gates and the streets of gold you have been waiting for. It is even better than you thought. We won't dwell on the material used to make the seventy-yard-thick wall or the streets made of gold, because it is a bit overwhelming to delve into all the details. But let's touch on the foundations of the city. If the twelve layers are of equal size, then each one is two stories high, made of insanely rare and precious stones.

Let's identify the clear contrast here. When Jesus entered into the first earth, he did so by humble means. He was born to a poor family in a cave used for farm animals. He did not own or even rent a home and would have died with only the clothes on his back if the soldiers hadn't stripped him naked. He came to identify with our physical poverty and spiritual struggle. In the days to come, though, when we enter into his world, the new earth, where he reigns as King, Jesus is righteously rich beyond words, and the city he has created will reflect his vast capacity. It will be breathtaking.

This is what John wrote of this grand city:

> I did not see a temple in the city, because the Lord God Almighty and the Lamb are its temple. The city does not need the sun or the moon to shine on it, for the glory of God gives it light, and the Lamb is its lamp. The nations will walk by its light, and the kings of the earth will bring their splendor into it. On no day will its gates ever be shut, for there will be no night there. The glory and honor of the nations will be brought into it. Nothing impure will ever enter it, nor will anyone who does what is shameful or deceitful, but only those whose names are written in the Lamb's book of life.
>
> —REVELATION 21:22–27

John seemed almost surprised that there is no temple in this city. If you remember your Old Testament teaching, the temple was very important throughout Israel's history. Created so God could live among his people, the temple of the Old Testament was used to sequester God's presence from the people because of their sin. But in the new city, there will be no more sin, and God will freely walk among us as he did with Adam and Eve.

Next John wrote that the city won't need the sun or the moon to provide it light. There may be a new sun and a new moon used outside of this city, but they will not be needed inside. Instead, the glory of God will provide a radiant beam to give us all the light we need in the city all the time. I don't have a clue what this will be like, but I am crazy excited about seeing and experiencing it.

John then tells us there will be no night in the new city, and at no time will the gates ever be shut. Gates are shut at night to keep evil out, but since there will be no night and, most important, no evil—since it will have been cast into the lake of fire—there will be no need ever to shut the gates. And since the only residents in this city will be those whose names are in the Book of Life and who have been freed to live in the light, there will also no longer be any sin. The city—and the whole new earth, for that matter—will be a sin-free zone.

John wrapped up his description of this grand city with my favorite part of all:

> Then the angel showed me the river of the water of life, as clear as crystal, flowing from the throne of God and of the Lamb down the middle of the great street of the city. On each side of the river stood the tree of life, bearing twelve crops of fruit, yielding its fruit every month. And the leaves of the tree are for the healing of the nations. No longer will there be any curse. The throne of God and of the Lamb will be in the city, and his servants will serve him. They will see his face, and his name will

be on their foreheads. There will be no more night. They will not need the light of a lamp or the light of the sun, for the Lord God will give them light. And they will reign for ever and ever.

—REVELATION 22:1–5

Imagine: a crystal clear river containing the same water Jesus offered the woman at the well (John 4:10–14). It doesn't just quench thirst, but it sustains life eternally. For centuries people such as Juan Ponce de León searched for the Fountain of Youth. Turns out it is not in the islands of Bimini but right smack-dab in the center of the New Jerusalem. This just might be something to see!

On either side of the river will be two identical trees—not just any random variety of trees but the Tree of Life from the original garden of Eden, bearing fruit that gives eternal life. We will have free and unlimited access to the fruit of the tree Adam and Eve ignored. We will sink our mouths full of healthy, resurrected teeth into that fruit and savor a *hint* of eternity in every bite.

What about the other tree from the garden of Eden? The Tree of the Knowledge of Good and Evil is nowhere to be found in John's description of the new city. And I believe that is intentional. That tree was put in the garden originally to give Adam and Eve a choice to follow God or not. When all things are made new, we will have already made our choice on the old earth between the life God offers and a life relying on our own knowledge. The tree will no longer have any purpose. The serpent will have been locked up for good with no possible access to slither his way back into this garden again. Yay, God!

And then, the best part of all, we will finally see God face-to-face.

In ancient times criminals were banished from the presence of the king (2 Samuel 14:24). We were once criminals and enemies of God and were banished from his presence. But no longer will this be our condition. We will be pardoned through faith in Christ and therefore no longer be prohibited from being in his presence. At this point we will be able to gaze directly into his eyes. John tells us here that we will receive a mark on our foreheads that bears Christ's name. I have never been big on tattoos. I just can't decide what permanent mark I would want to place on my body and am not sure how it would look on me when I'm ninety years old. Well, this is one tattoo I am prepared to take with great honor. This mark will basically remind us that, as crazy as it may seem, we belong here.

LIFE FOREVER

As I pondered all these beautiful and amazing things God has in store for us in Life Forever, it dawned on me—this great river flowing from the throne of God will certainly rival the great Niagara Falls. As it turns out, my trip with my mother has not been canceled, just postponed. And the trip is paid for in full, not by her son, but by the Son of God. And it won't be for just three days in a rented hotel, but forever as a permanent residence. My mother will not be able to wiggle her way out this time by dying. Death will have been thrown into the lake of fire, never to worry us again. Mom will be so embarrassed by the accommodations Jesus provides for her.

I envision Jesus looking her in the eye and tenderly saying, "Now, Ruth, you need to get used to this. I died to make this available for you. You are a daughter of the Father and have received your inheritance as promised."

And so it will be for all of us who believe.

Will I see you there? God makes it abundantly clear throughout Scripture that it is his desire that all would be saved and experience this glorious future he has prepared for us. There is room for everyone, but God only wants those there who want to be there. Do you want to be there? Then, before it is too late, you need to let him know. There is only one entry door, and his name is Jesus Christ (John 10:9).

THERE IS ONLY ONE ENTRY DOOR, AND HIS NAME IS JESUS CHRIST.

We may never meet in this life, you and I, but if you have decided to say yes to Jesus, I look forward to meeting you in the life to come—Life Forever. You will find me by the river. I hope you stop by. I would like to introduce you to my mom.

Q&A on Life Forever

Will rewards be given out?

THE BIBLE IS PRETTY CLEAR ABOUT THIS QUESTION. Yes, believers will receive rewards that will be given out at the beginning of life on the new earth—in Life Forever. Believers will be judged in the end (Romans 14:10), but not in the same way that unbelievers will be judged before the Great White Throne. This judgment will not be to determine our salvation or entrance through the pearly gates but instead will determine the rewards we will receive for how we lived our lives during Life Now.

Paul stated this clearly in his inspired writings to the believers at Corinth:

> For we must all appear before the judgment seat of Christ, so that each of us may receive what is due us for the things done while in the body, whether good or bad.
>
> —2 CORINTHIANS 5:10; SEE ALSO
> COLOSSIANS 3:23–24; REVELATION 22:12

This wasn't the first time Paul talked about this to the Corinthian church. In his first letter he wrote:

The one who plants and the one who waters have one purpose, and they will each be rewarded according to their own labor. . . . For no one can lay any foundation other than the one already laid, which is Jesus Christ. If anyone builds on this foundation using gold, silver, costly stones, wood, hay or straw, their work will be shown for what it is, because the Day will bring it to light. It will be revealed with fire, and the fire will test the quality of each person's work. If what has been built survives, the builder will receive a reward. If it is burned up, the builder will suffer loss but yet will be saved—even though only as one escaping through the flames.

—1 CORINTHIANS 3:8, 11–15

The word *Day* in this passage refers to the day when Christ returns and this judgment takes place. The deeds we have done that matter to God (signified here by gold, silver, and precious stones) will be rewarded. The deeds we have done for ourselves, that don't match God's priorities (like wood, hay, and straw) will count for nothing. Paul projected there will be some believers at this judgment whose total contributions in this life will be completely burned to nothing but who will still be saved because they laid their lives down on the foundation of Christ. I don't want to be that guy, do you?

Scripture says that in this weighing of our lives' choices we will be judged in three areas:

1. *The content of our work*

Jesus informs us, "The Son of Man is going to come in his Father's glory with his angels, and then he will reward each person according to what they have done" (Matthew 16:27).

This should cause us to look long and hard at our to-do list for each day. In the end we will regret simply waking up every day and living it for ourselves. James 1:27 says it is very important that believers help out widows and orphans in their distress. We all have a tremendous amount of responsibility, but according to James, this is just one example of what really matters to God. In Luke 14 Jesus tells us he really wants us from time to time to invite people over for dinner who cannot repay us or advance our position in life, such as the poor, the blind, and the lame. If you do, Jesus said, "You will be blessed. Although they cannot repay you, you will be repaid at the resurrection of the righteous" (Luke 14:14). These are just two items we would be wise to make a priority in our schedules sooner rather than later.

2. *The words we speak*

Jesus is not hiding his expectations for us: "But I tell you that everyone will have to give account on the day of judgment for every empty word they have spoken" (Matthew 12:36).

Ouch! That's a pretty stiff challenge. Even the casual words we throw out without much thought come under God's scrutiny. On a positive note, even if we don't have lots of money to give away to the hurting, downtrodden, and poor, words of encouragement count greatly in God's book. Be conscious of that as you go through the rest of your day. I know I will. I just hope I remember it for tomorrow and the next day.

3. *The motives of our hearts*

Therefore judge nothing before the appointed time; wait until the Lord comes. He will bring to light what is hidden in darkness and will expose the motives of the heart. At that time each will receive their praise from God (1 Corinthians 4:5; see also Ephesians 6:8).

It isn't just what we do, but the motive for which we do it. I can't judge your motives; you can't judge mine (Matthew 7:1–5). In the verse right before Paul's admonition to the Corinthians, he wrote, "It is the Lord who judges me" (1 Corinthians 4:5).

If you are a believer, you will face a judgment where your choices made in Life Now will be weighed on these three bases, and you will receive the appropriate reward from a just and loving God. These rewards will likely determine the quality of your life in the new kingdom, as well as your position.

For years I just thought everyone would be the same in the afterlife, but that is not what the Bible teaches. So, as you build up your divine 401(k) account, remember Jesus' advice:

Do not store up for yourselves treasures on earth, where moths and vermin destroy, and where thieves break in and steal. But store up for yourselves treasures in heaven, where moths and vermin do not destroy, and where thieves do not break in and steal.

—MATTHEW 6:19–20

Will there be pets in heaven?

Our family enjoyed the company of a beagle named Lady for eighteen years. Without question, she was the most loyal creature I ever encountered. There hasn't been even a close second. If heaven could be earned through merit, Lady stands a much better chance than I do of getting into the new kingdom. So, will she, or any beagle for that matter, walk the new earth with believers in Jesus?

Let's start at the beginning for clues. Revelation 21–22 has a theme identical to Genesis 1–2. God's vision for life on the new earth is a restoration of his vision that was lost on this earth. So we can look at these two chapters in Genesis and safely conclude that what was there at that time will be re-created.

During creation, after God separated the waters below from the sky above on the second day, he filled them with all kinds of birds and fish.

> And God said, "Let the water teem with living creatures, and let birds fly above the earth across the vault of the sky." So God created the great creatures of the sea and every living thing with which the water teems and that moves about in it, according to their kinds, and every winged bird according to its kind. And God saw that it was good. God blessed them and said, "Be fruitful and increase in number and fill the water in the seas, and let the birds increase on the earth."
>
> —Genesis 1:20–22

After God created the land on the third day, he filled it with all kinds of creatures on the sixth day.

And God said, "Let the land produce living creatures according to their kinds: the livestock, the creatures that move along the ground, and the wild animals, each according to its kind." And it was so. God made the wild animals according to their kinds, the livestock according to their kinds, and all the creatures that move along the ground according to their kinds. And God saw that it was good.

—GENESIS 1:24–25

Creatures of the sea and oceans and the creatures of the dry land are on this earth as a part of God's vision. It is safe to assume they will be a part of the new earth. Actually, Isaiah received a vision of the new earth, and he most definitely found various kinds of animals present in it—and behaving in a most interesting way.

"The wolf and the lamb will feed together,
and the lion will eat straw like the ox,
and dust will be the serpent's food.
They will neither harm nor destroy
on all my holy mountain,"
says the LORD.

—ISAIAH 65:25

Not only will there be animals in the new kingdom, but they will get along. Because there will be no death, there will be no predators. Frankly, I am not sure how God is going to manage to control population growth, particularly among rabbits, but I will leave that up to his infinite ingenuity.

Isaiah gives us even more truth about what we can expect in our future dwelling in chapter 11:

> The wolf will live with the lamb,
> the leopard will lie down with the goat,
> the calf and the lion and the yearling together;
> and a little child will lead them.
>
> —Isaiah 11:6

This not only suggests that we will have pets in the new kingdom, but the variety of pets will drastically expand. We will not only have dogs, cats, goldfish, gerbils, and parrots for pets, but this verse leads me to believe we may be able to swim with a pool of piranhas or walk with a jaguar. Yikes!

Will my beagle, Lady, be there? Will your pet be there? There is no indication in Scripture that Lady will be re-created, but it certainly isn't outside the realm of God's amazing power and lavish love for us.

Will we keep our memories or regrets from Life Now?

After living on this earth now for more than half a century, I have accumulated a bucket-load of memories, most of them good, but some of them horrific. How about you? When I enter the gates of the new city and receive the keys to the place Jesus built for me, will my memories and regrets come with me?

I am pretty sure the answer is no. John's vivid vision of life in New Jerusalem tells us, "'He will wipe every tear from their eyes. There will be no more death' or mourning or crying or pain, for the old order of things has passed away" (Revelation 21:4).

As Jesus' index finger swipes across our cheeks, I believe the memories of our previous life on the old earth will be gone. The

Great White Throne judgment for unbelievers takes place right before Jesus does this for us. I imagine the tears rolling down our faces at that point will be for those we knew who just wouldn't seek or accept Jesus in this life and were cast into the lake of fire. It would be hard for me to carry this visual memory with me into eternity without letting it weigh me down in sadness.

Frankly, I am okay with this divinely induced amnesia. Someone wisely said, "When your memories are bigger than your dreams, your life is over." Life on the new earth carries such big dreams for us. Listen to Isaiah's vision of the kind of life that awaits us:

> See, I will create
>> new heavens and a new earth.
> The former things will not be remembered,
>> nor will they come to mind.
> But be glad and rejoice forever
>> in what I will create,
>> for I will create Jerusalem to be a delight
>> and its people a joy.
> I will rejoice over Jerusalem
>> and take delight in my people;
> the sound of weeping and of crying
>> will be heard in it no more.

—ISAIAH 65:17–19

Isaiah reinforces John's declaration and then immediately adds the word *but*. But, he says, be glad and rejoice forever: we have so many new memories to make that will not be intermingled with things that make us weep.

Will there be marriages and family in God's new kingdom?

I have been married to my wife, Rozanne, for thirty-five years and counting. If she will continue to have me, I plan to finish out all my days on this old earth with her, not only because I promised I would, but because I can't imagine life without her. We have been together since we first started sitting in church together at the age of fifteen. We also have four grown children, two of whom are now married, and two grandchildren (with many more on the way, I am sure). Pure and simple, my marriage and my family are the core of my life. It is hard for me to imagine us not being a family in the new life to come.

I have had an amazing experience with my family. Others, not so much. There are some who never got married in this life but wanted to. There are couples who were unable to bear children. Then there are the families that are marred with almost unbearable dysfunction and pain. Finally, there are broken and blended families as a result of divorce that makes this subject way more complicated.

So as I approach this question regarding marriage, I once again look to God's original design in Genesis 1–2. In most cases there is continuity between what it was like then and what it will be like on the new earth. Adam and Eve were married and had children. They were a family. Therefore, it seems safe to suggest there will be marriage after we experience our resurrection.

This would hold true if Jesus didn't trump this notion. During Jesus' ministry on earth, a group of religious leaders tried to get Jesus in trouble with a question regarding marriage. They really didn't care much about Jesus' answer. You see, they didn't believe in the resurrection of the dead and were trying to get him to admit in public that he did.

They posed a scenario where a woman had been married seven times because each of her previous husbands had died. (It sounds to me as if she might have been poisoning their food, but the text doesn't say.) Finally, the woman died. Here is the question they asked Jesus to get him to take their bait: "Now then, at the resurrection, whose wife will she be of the seven, since all of them were married to her?" (Matthew 22:28).

Not only did Jesus boldly admit that he believed in the resurrection of the dead, but he also answered the question about marriage after we receive our resurrected bodies:

> Jesus replied, "You are in error because you do not know the Scriptures or the power of God. At the resurrection people will neither marry nor be given in marriage; they will be like the angels in heaven. But about the resurrection of the dead—have you not read what God said to you, 'I am the God of Abraham, the God of Isaac, and the God of Jacob'? He is not the God of the dead but of the living."
>
> —MATTHEW 22:29–32

Jesus couldn't have said it plainer: "At the resurrection people will neither marry nor be given in marriage." As we look through the Scriptures for God's bigger vision, we see that, in fact, there is a single marriage in the new kingdom—the marriage between Christ and the church. Paul said that our marriages on the old earth foreshadow the ultimate marriage between Christ and his church.

"For this reason a man will leave his father and mother and be united to his wife, and the two will become one flesh." This is a profound mystery—but I am talking about Christ and the church.

—Ephesians 5:31–32

True confession. This doesn't really work for me. While my wife loves me and lets me know daily she loves being married to me, I think this idea of being married to Jesus works more for her than it does for me. I don't blame her. But as a guy, this concept doesn't connect with me.

Here is what I am left with. I must trust the good and gracious God, who has brought me to this point through his sheer grace. When I am sitting at the wedding supper of the Lamb (Revelation 19:9), I am confident it will not only make great sense but will also exceed my expectations.

The text doesn't say Rozanne and I won't know each other and still be best of friends. We will likely be even better friends, because my sin nature—which still from time to time does her wrong—will be completely gone. I do like that idea, the idea of not having to say "I'm sorry" for the umpteenth time. I am assuming the relationship I will continue to have with Rozanne—at least as very close friends—will be the same as what I will have with my children.

It appears there will not be millions of families on the new earth, just one very big united family under the headship of Christ. The more I think about it, the more I am liking it. We'll just have to wait and see.

What will our resurrected bodies be like?

Here is a question whose answer I know lots of people are interested in knowing. The answer is addressed explicitly in 1 Corinthians 15:35–55. Paul began this section of his writings with the $64,000 question: "But someone will ask, 'How are the dead raised? With what kind of body will they come?'" (v. 35). Paul immediately answered:

> What you sow does not come to life unless it dies. When you sow, you do not plant the body that will be, but just a seed, perhaps of wheat or of something else. But God gives it a body as he has determined, and to each kind of seed he gives its own body.
>
> —1 CORINTHIANS 15:36–38

Paul compared the resurrection to planting. Our current bodies are the seeds for our new bodies. This seed determines the kind of body the sprouting plant will grow into, yet it won't be the same as the seed planted. I think this means we each will have a body that looks like the one we have now, but it won't be exactly the same. It will be better. That is what Paul wrote next:

> The body that is sown is perishable, it is raised imperishable; it is sown in dishonor, it is raised in glory; it is sown in weakness, it is raised in power; it is sown a natural body, it is raised a spiritual body.
>
> —1 CORINTHIANS 15:42–44

With our current bodies we experience aches and pains, the effects of aging, susceptibility to disease, and the inevitability of death. Our new bodies will not contain or experience any of these defects caused by sin. We will be without sin. That means no more cancer, no more diabetes, no more wheelchairs, no more blindness, no more deafness, no more chronic pain, no fear of death . . . because we will never die again.

I love the comparison Paul made between our natural and spiritual bodies:

> The first man was of the dust of the earth; the second man is of heaven. As was the earthly man, so are those who are of the earth; and as is the heavenly man, so also are those who are of heaven. And just as we have borne the image of the earthly man, so shall we bear the image of the heavenly man.
>
> —1 Corinthians 15:47–49

Our natural bodies are born of Adam. Our spiritual bodies will be born of the second Adam, who is Jesus. Our resurrected bodies will bear the image of Jesus' resurrected body. What do we know about Jesus' resurrected body?

1. *Jesus looked the same in resurrection as he did before death.* We know this because his disciples and followers who saw him recognized him. I assume we will look the same as we did in our earthly bodies, minus anything that might be unhealthy, internally or externally. That should mean we will be the appropriate weight for our body size and type. Can I get an amen?

2. We assume *Jesus' new body came back at the same age as when he died.* I don't think this means if we die at ten we

will perpetually stay ten and if we die at ninety we will forever look as though we are ninety. Actually, we just don't know. Some serious thinkers about theology have suggested we will have bodies that represent our prime years, which are somewhere in our late twenties to early thirties.[1] I can live with that.

3. *Jesus came back as a man.* I think there will be gender in heaven, and we will each maintain the gender we had in our natural bodies.

4. *Jesus had the ability to physically appear and disappear and go through locked doors* (Luke 24:31; John 20:19). We are not totally sure this feature will carry over to us, but it is reasonable to think we will since we will bear his image. How cool is the thought of that?

We can also look at the bodies of Adam and Eve before the fall to get some clues as to what we might be able to expect. The most alarming observation for most people is that they were naked. Yikes! Yet, in the book of Revelation we are told of people wearing white robes. We can't really know about this, but one thing we do know for sure is that we will not feel ashamed or vulnerable in the same way Adam and Eve did not feel ashamed before they partook of the Tree of the Knowledge of Good and Evil. That is a big improvement over our current condition on this earth.

We will also maintain our ethnic identities. We don't really know what ethnic makeup Adam and Eve had in their bodies, but we did all come from them originally, so it's fair to say we will likely maintain the genetic makeup we've been given in Life Now.

106

Read this beautiful scene from the book of Revelation about our life to come:

> After this I looked, and there before me was a great multitude that no one could count, from every nation, tribe, people and language, standing before the throne and before the Lamb. They were wearing white robes and were holding palm branches in their hands. And they cried out in a loud voice: "Salvation belongs to our God, who sits on the throne, and to the Lamb."
>
> —Revelation 7:9–10)

We live in a time of great racial tension. It has always been this way; it shall always be this way until this old world comes to an end and Jesus returns. On the new earth we will not all look or sound the same. Diversity will still exist, but we will be completely unified. How can this be? In our diversity we will experience unity under the name of Jesus, who sits on the throne. It will be a beautiful thing.

What will we eat?

In Jesus' model prayer we are instructed to ask God to "give us this day our daily bread" (Matthew 6:11). Food and drink are essential to our survival and sustainability in our natural bodies. But eating and drinking often go way beyond the basic requirements for life. Gathering with family and friends to share a meal may be some of the most enriching experiences in life. Consider the one thing Jesus asked us to do over and over again: remember his death until he comes, or share communion as he did with his disciples at the Last Supper. Jesus brings us around the dinner table (1 Corinthians 11:26).

As we ponder eternal life on the new earth, will eating and drinking be essential, necessary, or even possible in our spiritual bodies? The answer is a resounding, confident *yes*.

We observe Jesus eating in his resurrected body (Luke 24:40–43; John 21:4–14; Acts 10:40–41). Jesus clearly demonstrated that the spiritual body is capable of eating and drinking.

Jesus also told his disciples explicitly that we will eat and drink in the new kingdom.

> For I tell you I will not drink again from the fruit of the vine until the kingdom of God comes. . . . And I confer on you a kingdom, just as my Father conferred one on me, so that you may eat and drink at my table in my kingdom and sit on thrones, judging the twelve tribes of Israel.
>
> —LUKE 22:18, 29–30

You don't need to go to seminary to know how to interpret the plain words of Jesus. We will eat and drink and share meals in the new kingdom. John gives us a heads-up on one of the invitations we have already received. Jesus has invited all of us who accepted his free gift of eternal life in Life Now to sit at his table:

> Then the angel said to me, "Write this: Blessed are those who are invited to the wedding supper of the Lamb!" And he added, "These are the true words of God."
>
> —REVELATION 19:9

What will our diet consist of? Isaiah describes the spread from the banquet above:

> On this mountain the LORD Almighty will prepare
> a feast of rich food for all peoples,
> a banquet of aged wine—
> the best of meats and the finest of wines.
>
> —ISAIAH 25:6

Now, that is my kind of meal! Add some potatoes au gratin, a few marinated Brussels sprouts, topped off with a little crème brûlée and a cappuccino for dessert, and I'm in heaven—oh wait! I *will* be. There is only one major problem.

As we go back to the garden and peer into God's original vision he is now seeking to restore, Adam and Eve didn't eat meat (Genesis 1:29–30). It wasn't until after the flood that God gave humanity permission to consume meat from animals. God said to Noah:

> Everything that lives and moves about will be food for you. Just
> as I gave you the green plants, I now give you everything.
>
> —GENESIS 9:3

We are clearly told that in God's new, eternal kingdom, "there will be no more death" (Revelation 21:4). Since this declaration is not limited to humans but extends to animals, it is safe to assume the diet on the new earth will be vegetarian. Homegrown fruits and vegetables might be rather tasty. And don't forget: pastas and bread are still on the menu.

What about Isaiah's words about the best of meats? Maybe there is something I am missing here, and there *will* be the best of meats sitting before our table each day. How does that work with there being no death? We won't know for sure until we get there, I suppose. Here is what we do know for sure: we will have unlimited access to the Tree of Life and to the water of life, and these two things will not only satisfy our hunger and thirst but sustain our eternal life. This takes the phrase "An apple a day keeps the doctor away" to a whole new level.

We will also have a seat at Jesus' table. We will not have to take a piece of bread or a cup to remember him anymore. The Bible says we only practice communion "until he comes" (1 Corinthians 11:26). All we need to do now is look up. Jesus will be sitting at the end of the table. Bon appetit!

What will a day in the life on the new earth be like?

Essentially, it will be like a day here on the old earth, without the curse and with the very presence of God among us. That's a pretty big difference, isn't it?

First, there will be rest and sleep in heaven (Hebrews 4:1–4; Revelation 14:13). In many ways, this whole salvation experience is to enable us to enter into a life of rest with God. And for the most important point of all, there will be coffee in the morning! Can I get an amen?

There will also be meaningful work for everyone. In the garden before the fall, God partnered with Adam to manage the earth under his authority (Genesis 1:28). I believe this responsibility will continue on the new earth, but without the frustration caused by the curse, since it will have been lifted (Revelation 22:3). Some of us will need to be reassigned. I don't see the need for law enforcement or armies, but there will be plenty of other things to do. There will be much room for creativity, inventing, and learning in our new digs.

There will also be times set aside for scrumptious meals with family and friends, as we discovered earlier. We will each have a place within the city limits to have people over. No tears will be shed but many evenings will be full of belly laughs (Luke 6:21). Neighborhood life will be vibrant, and many evenings will be spent whiling away the hours with friends.

There will also be travel outside of the New Jerusalem to explore the new seven—or seven thousand—wonders of the world God paints this go-round. I can only imagine how we will get around based on the potential abilities in our new bodies. There will be time for hobbies like knitting, biking, kayaking, bird-watching, gardening for sure, and golfing (my personal favorite). I don't imagine hunting will be on the list, unless it involves hunting something other than animals to kill. Sorry, guys!

The biggest improvement of all will be the church services. There won't be a temple to meet in. God himself will be there and act as the temple (Revelation 21:22). There will be no more sermons inviting people to confess their sins and receive Jesus. There will be no more sin. There will be no more healing services necessary, because there will be no more hurt, dysfunction, or disease (Revelation 21:4). Church services will purely consist of worship and gratitude for what God has done for us. There will be a bunch of "someone pinch me" moments, as what we have sinks in every single day. Worship in the actual presence of God. Maybe I'll be asked to do the sermon, if there is one. Sounds a bit intimidating. Or perhaps we will simply sit at the feet of Jesus and listen to him tell stories about the Father's great love for us. He was great at that when he walked on the earth. Remember the parables?

You know, Life Now on this ol' earth has been pretty busy. We just don't have enough time for everything we want to do and all the people we want to meet and spend time with. We don't have time to linger or smell the roses. But life on the new earth will be much different. Time will be on our side.

We may never get to meet in this life, but we will definitely have the margin to meet in the life to come. I sure hope we do. Maybe we can meet up at the pearly gates or take a stroll down the streets of gold or share a piece a fruit on a park bench next to the Tree of Life or sit next to each other at a dinner with Jesus or, if you are into golf as I am, maybe we can get in a round. No cheating allowed, but plenty of mulligans available. It is going to be great! Thank you, Jesus!

LIFE NOW

CHAPTER SIX

Until Then

IN MY FAMILY, WE'VE MADE VACATIONS A MAJOR priority. Even with our four children now grown, we have set a vision to gather them at least every other year, along with their spouses and the grandchildren, for the best trip we can put together with the resources we have. We never surprise our children with a last-minute trip. Rather, we opt to tell them months in advance. Why?

The power of anticipation.

When our kids were little, every day for months they had the opportunity to look forward to our annual family trip. I would be sure to go over every detail, day by day, of the places we would go and the things we would do. If the trip required a long drive to Colorado for skiing, I would tell them about the hotel we were staying at on the way that served breakfast for dinner and had an indoor swimming pool. They would find themselves daydreaming about ordering pancakes for dinner or skiing for the first time or going down the new roller coaster ride. They would no doubt talk

115

it up among their friends from school with a sense of satisfaction that our family had a plan.

Around the dinner table at night, we would say, "Only forty-five days until we take off. . . . Only forty-four days until we take off. . . ." The night before we were to take off, sleep was always a bit restless due to the pent-up anticipation.

There is sustaining power in anticipation. What was true for our children is true for the Christian and our trip into the afterlife, but on a much grander scale. The Bible calls this anticipation our hope. The writer of the book of Hebrews recounted the tremendous hope the Old Testament saints found in anticipation of their journey to the promised city in the New Jerusalem:

> All these people were still living by faith when they died. They did not receive the things promised; they only saw them and welcomed them from a distance, admitting that they were foreigners and strangers on earth. People who say such things show that they are looking for a country of their own. If they had been thinking of the country they had left, they would have had opportunity to return. Instead, they were longing for a better country—a heavenly one. Therefore God is not ashamed to be called their God, for he has prepared a city for them.
>
> —HEBREWS 11:13–16

Hope is one of the most powerful things a human can possess. So here is the final question we must answer, given all we have to look forward to . . .

HOW DO WE LIVE UNTIL THEN?

This is a question that is central for those who believe, those who have hope, those seeking to live in light of heaven. In some ways, it is what sets Christians apart from the rest of the world, as our choices and the testimony of our actions reflect our answer to this question, our response to the future God is calling us to.

So it's not surprising that many early church leaders—and even Jesus himself—spoke to this. Peter hit the topic head-on in his second letter:

> But the day of the Lord will come like a thief. The heavens will disappear with a roar; the elements will be destroyed by fire, and the earth and everything done in it will be laid bare.
>
> Since everything will be destroyed in this way, what kind of people ought you to be? You ought to live holy and godly lives as you look forward to the day of God and speed its coming. That day will bring about the destruction of the heavens by fire, and the elements will melt in the heat. But in keeping with his promise we are looking forward to a new heaven and a new earth, where righteousness dwells.
>
> —2 PETER 3:10–13

The destruction of our existing earth will not be a pretty sight—cataclysmic, actually. This will make every apocalyptic movie humans have created seem like an episode of *Sesame Street*. But it doesn't end with total destruction.

Notice Peter said, "We are looking forward to a new heaven and a new earth." Here is the power of anticipation. So, in light of the promise of God for your future life, "What kind of people ought you to be?" Peter asked.

The answer is plainly stated here and throughout the New Testament. This is how we should live until then: live holy and godly lives, live unafraid, live by faith, encourage each other, be witnesses, and pray.

Live Holy and Godly Lives

Why should we be compelled to live holy and godly lives in light of our future home? Peter stated the reason at the end of verse 13. The new heaven and earth, in which believers will reside, is the place "where righteousness dwells." Peter admonished us to begin living now as we will live then—holy and godly.

The word *holy* means "separate" and suggests that we live our lives in a distinctly different way from the rest of the world. What does that look like exactly? Paul graphically drew the distinction in his writing to the Philippian believers:

Their [enemies of the cross] destiny is destruction, their god is their stomach, and their glory is in their shame. Their mind is set on earthly things. But our citizenship is in heaven. And we eagerly await a Savior from there, the Lord Jesus Christ, who, by the power that enables him to bring everything under his control, will transform our lowly bodies so that they will be like his glorious body.

—PHILIPPIANS 3:19–21

Those who don't believe in Jesus or desire to be residents in his eternal kingdom have nothing to look forward to after death.

Their god is their stomach, and therefore they bow down to the extraction of as much pleasure from this short life as possible. "Their mind is set on earthly things."

Jesus told a parable of a guy who was exactly like this. He kept gaining more and more wealth, so much so that it was overflowing and he had no place to store it all. What did he do with all this excess? He decided to build bigger barns to store all his wealth for his personal consumption. What was this rich man's philosophy of life?

> And I'll say to myself, "You have plenty of grain laid up for many years. Take life easy; eat, drink and be merry."
>
> —LUKE 12:19

A person who doesn't believe in God has no one to answer to except himself. Essentially, he has no moral absolutes, rights, or wrongs. The logical conclusion, then, is to "eat, drink and be merry." Consume yourself in selfish, pleasurable living with regard to no one else. Drink yourself into a drunken stupor so your mind is numb to the meaninglessness of life.

Paul agreed with this logic in his first letter to the believers in Corinth:

> If the dead are not raised,
>
> "Let us eat and drink,
> for tomorrow we die."
>
> —1 CORINTHIANS 15:32

119

But we have a different destiny. Jesus did rise from the dead, and so will we. Believers in Jesus essentially have passports with no expiration date, signifying our citizenship is in heaven. As the old gospel song declares, "This world is not my home; I'm just a-passin' through." We are from a place where righteousness dwells, and we will act today as ambassadors of our homeland.

Let's go back to Philippians 3:20. Notice Paul said we live this godly way as we "eagerly await a Savior from there." There's that daily anticipation filling the hearts of followers of Jesus that motivates us to live now as we will for eternity, where evil, greed, lying, cheating, hoarding, deceiving, destroying, undermining, and killing have no rights and will be stopped at the border every single time.

In the parable, God said to the rich man who rejected him, "You fool! This very night your life will be demanded from you. Then who will get what you have prepared for yourself?" (Luke 12:20). When our focus is only on the here and now, we naturally gravitate toward storing up temporary plenty that is only good for Life Now. But when our eyes are opened and we see the expanse of eternity and all God has put into place, we realize the uselessness of reveling in what feels pleasurable on such a short-term basis. Suddenly, God's desire for us to lead holy and godly lives, full of vision for our ultimate futures, surpasses the smallness of what the world offers. And when we choose him, we will one day hear God say to us, "Enter into these gates to enjoy the fullness of your inheritance forever, which I have prepared for you. Welcome home!"

Live Unafraid

Jesus himself gives us our second piece of advice on how we should live until then. In John 14, Jesus' disciples had just learned of his coming departure and how they wouldn't be able to go with him right away. Jesus turned to them in this anxious moment and gave them these assuring words of hope: "Do not let your hearts be troubled. You believe in God; believe also in me" (v. 1).

Do not let your hearts be troubled. What exactly does that look like, and how can we help being troubled?

When after my mother's death I was struggling with my belief in heaven and the afterlife, I believe God himself arranged for me to have an all-day meeting with a popular theologian by the name of Jim Packer, who had just finished a book on biblical hope.[1] I was working on an assessment tool that helped people measure where they were against a biblical portrait of Christ at the time, and had identified thirty core characteristics of Christ.[2] *Christianity Today,* from the Chicago area, took an interest in this tool and graciously gave me a few one-on-one days with their resident theologian, who happened to be Dr. Packer, to give me feedback.

I was already sitting in the small conference room when he arrived. He was carrying a manila folder and a Bible. When he sat down, he opened up the folder, and there I saw my work with red ink all over it. For one, I couldn't believe he had taken this much time to pore over my work. For another, it was pretty frightening when I realized just how much feedback he had in store for me to hear. He immediately dove in with a surprising summary.

"Randy, you have done excellent work here. I like all thirty of the core characteristics. They are spot-on and biblical. However, you left out one that must be present. You left out hope. If you add this virtue to your list, I can wholeheartedly support this tool."

After he convincingly proved to me that hope was an essential Christian virtue, I asked Dr. Packer to define hope. Without even a blink of an eye, he blurted out, in his rich British accent, "I can cope with hope." The words cut deep. I wasn't coping well with the loss of my mother, and I could sense he knew something was wrong deep inside me.

I asked Dr. Packer how one secures this virtue of hope.

With a brief rub of his chin, he said, "For a Christian to have hope, they must believe in the promise, and they must trust the One making the promise. The promise is eternal life with God in the new kingdom. The One making the promise is Jesus."

> "FOR A CHRISTIAN TO HAVE HOPE, THEY MUST BELIEVE IN THE PROMISE, AND THEY MUST TRUST THE ONE MAKING THE PROMISE."
>
> —DR. PACKER

He went on to explain that Jesus fulfilled his promise to provide the only way to the Father when he died on the cross for our sins (John 14:6). Now we are being asked to trust him, to put off any fear and anxiety, to believe he will come back and personally take us to the Father, just as he said he would.

Dr. Packer's words spoke directly to my bruised soul. My heart was troubled, and I couldn't find a way to experience Jesus' offer in John 14. That day Dr. Packer taught me that if I were ever to have this brand of hope, I couldn't just will it.

I needed to get to know Christ better and be utterly convinced that he was who he said he was and that what he taught was true. Then I needed to dive deeper into what he promised about eternal life.

Hope is completely tethered to our belief system. That was a new idea for me: a radical idea that took me on what has proven to be a very effective journey of instilling God's hope within me. If your heart is troubled, if you live in fear of the future, this will work for you as well.

Remember: the worst thing that can happen to us is death, and Jesus has that covered. So, how do we live now in light of our guaranteed future? We live without fear!

Live by Faith

Hebrews 11 opens with these beautiful words: "Now faith is confidence in what we hope for and assurance about what we do not see" (v. 1).

There is a distinct difference between faith and hope. In today's vernacular we might say, "I hope this happens," meaning "I really don't think it will happen, but I wish it would." This is not how the writers of the Bible used the term. As Dr. Packer alluded to in my conversation with him, biblical hope is based on what we *know* is going to happen.

- As believers, we *know* that when we die, our spirits go to be in the presence of God.
- We *know* that Jesus will return.
- We *know* we will receive resurrected bodies.
- We *know* he is creating a place for us.

- We *know* we will be residents in the new kingdom.
- We *know* we will live in God's kingdom forever and ever, with no possibility of pain, tears, illness, evil, or death again.

We don't see it now, but we have the assurance based on the One who made the promise—Jesus himself. Faith, on the other hand, is different. The writer of Hebrews gave us an example later in the chapter:

> By faith Abraham, when called to go to a place he would later receive as his inheritance, obeyed and went, even though he did not know where he was going.
>
> —HEBREWS 11:8

The writer was referring to Genesis 12, when God visited Abraham and told him to leave the comforts of his homeland. God invited him to begin walking with no earthly idea of where he would land. Abraham and Sarah decided to go. Why? Because they believed in the promises God gave them, and they "considered him faithful who made the promise" (v. 11).

Abraham believed God was going to give them a baby and build them into a great nation even though he was too old to have children and his wife was barren. His hope was in a tangible and overtly clear promise—a baby will be born. So, "by faith," he and his wife packed up their belongings and started walking one step at a time toward the unknown, waiting for God to give instruction.

God fulfilled his promise, and they had a child named Isaac.

But when Isaac was a teenager, God instructed Abraham to sacrifice him on an altar. The writer goes on to tells us:

> By faith Abraham, when God tested him, offered Isaac as a sacrifice. He who had embraced the promises was about to sacrifice his one and only son, even though God had said to him, "It is through Isaac that your offspring will be reckoned."
> —HEBREWS 11:17–18

What was going on in Abraham's mind that allowed him to do the unthinkable? The text above tells us he "embraced the promises." The next verse gives us a peek into Abraham's mind at the time:

> Abraham reasoned that God could even raise the dead, and so in a manner of speaking he did receive Isaac back from death.
> —HEBREWS 11:19)

Abraham's hope was anchored in God's promise on how his story would end. He trusted God to work out the details. Even though he had never seen a resurrection, he figured God would, by his mighty power, raise his son from the dead and keep his promise. Of course, as the flint knife was in downward motion God interrupted Abraham and provided a sacrifice in place of his son Isaac, a ram whose horns were caught in a thicket (Genesis 22:13).

With each step of faith, Abraham's relationship with God deepened, and he got greater insight into the One making the promises to him. With each promise that was fulfilled, Abraham began to realize the full promise of God for his life. It went way beyond what he originally thought. This was not only true of Abraham but also of the host of other Old Testament believers.

> All these people were still living by faith when they died. They did not receive the things promised; they only saw them and welcomed them from a distance, admitting that they were foreigners and strangers on earth. People who say such things show that they are looking for a country of their own. If they had been thinking of the country they had left, they would have had opportunity to return. Instead, they were longing for a better country—a heavenly one. Therefore God is not ashamed to be called their God, for he has prepared a city for them.
>
> —HEBREWS 11:13–16

These believers ultimately saw God's grander promise of a "heavenly" country. They were "looking forward to the city with foundations, whose architect and builder is God" (Hebrews 11:10). Their hope was the same as our hope, except we have a more vivid picture of it and thus should be even more encouraged to live today by faith.

Faith is trusting God today to follow through on his word even when we don't fully know what's around the next bend in the road. We find the courage to live by faith today because we have "confidence in what we hope for" in the future. We don't know about all the bends, turns, and detours in this life, but we do know the final outcome. And until then, we must choose to live by faith.

Encourage Each Other

It is easy to become discouraged in Life Now. So many things are out of our control. This is not only true for us today, but it was also true for the first-century believers. When Paul wrote a letter to the believers who made up the church in the city of Thessalonica, they had already received and fully embraced the teaching of Christ's second return, which would usher them into Life Forever, but they had somehow concluded that Christ was going to return in their lifetime and had gotten super concerned about the participation in the new kingdom of those who died before his return. Paul wrote these words to them concerning those who had already died, also addressing the fear they naturally had about their own deaths.

Brothers and sisters, we do not want you to be uninformed about those who sleep in death, so that you do not grieve like the rest of mankind, who have no hope. For we believe that Jesus died and rose again, and so we believe that God will bring with Jesus those who have fallen asleep in him. According to the Lord's word, we tell you that we who are still alive, who are left until the coming of the Lord, will certainly not precede those who have fallen asleep. For the Lord himself will come down from heaven, with a loud command, with the voice of the archangel and with the trumpet call of God, and the dead in Christ will rise first. After that, we who are still alive and are left will be caught up together with them in the clouds to meet the Lord in the air. And so we will be with the Lord forever. Therefore encourage one another with these words.

—1 THESSALONIANS 4:13–18

127

These words are just as much for us today as they were for those ancient followers. I lost hope when my mother died. Her ailment started with a little cough and a little pain, and before we knew it, she had passed away. For the next two years, every little cough, pain, or bump I felt or experienced brought me nothing but fear. *This could be it for me*, I thought.

As I read and studied the Scriptures, though, I began to know God better, and I began to trust these truths about what is to come when Jesus returns. And now the fear I experienced previously seems completely ludicrous. Yes, the journey to death may be challenging and even painful, but maybe not. I personally am praying that I go to sleep one night and wake up in the presence of Jesus. But no matter how it happens, through Christ I have already overcome death.

Some people obsess over dying; Christians need to obsess over living. Some people are riddled with fear; believers need to be riddled with joy. Our minds should be centered on God's promises, and when one of us struggles, the others should lift the struggling one up.

Our Christian fellowship should be constantly sprinkled with encouragement about the realities of our guaranteed future in Christ. We need to help one another pit our current troubles against the promise of eternity to gain perspective and find peace.

It's no secret that African slaves from earlier in American history lived horrific and demoralizing lives, with little hope of change. But even in the midst of what seemed so hopeless, they created spiritual songs that helped them "cope with hope" and kept their eyes fixed on the fact that this life of slavery was only temporary compared to the eternal life to come as sons and daughters of the King of kings.

While they sang these songs together in church gatherings as a community, they also sang them outside those gatherings while they were laboring, pointing their focus away from their earthly slavery and toward their coming freedom in Christ.[3]

We need to do the same today. Whenever a fellow believer is facing deep sorrow, unimaginable heartbreak, or trouble with little hope for relief, we need to gather around as a community of believers to encourage that individual, love that person, and remind them of their ultimate victory in Jesus.

We need to read and reread to one another the words Paul wrote to encourage the believers in his day:

> Therefore we do not lose heart. Though outwardly we are wasting away, yet inwardly we are being renewed day by day. For our light and momentary troubles are achieving for us an eternal glory that far outweighs them all. So we fix our eyes not on what is seen, but on what is unseen, since what is seen is temporary, but what is unseen is eternal.
>
> —2 CORINTHIANS 4:16–18

Be Witnesses

Remember the parable Jesus told about the rich man and Lazarus? After they both died, Lazarus's spirit went to Abraham's side, or paradise, and the rich man's spirit went to Hades. When the rich man realized there was absolutely no relief or way out, he called out to Abraham and made his passionate plea for Lazarus to be sent back from the dead to warn the rich man's family about what they would inevitably also experience in Hades. The afterlife is real for both the believer and the unbeliever. Lazarus may not have been sent back from the dead to speak to the rich man's family as requested, but we who are still alive, who really believe, should be compelled to tell others about the wonderful offer of Christ up until our last breath or Christ's return. Once we are gone, our opportunity to tell others will be gone as well.

This is the commission of Jesus on our lives. After his resurrection and before his ascension back to the Father in heaven, Jesus visited the disciples one last time. This is what Jesus said in that final gathering:

> But you will receive power when the Holy Spirit comes on you; and you will be my witnesses in Jerusalem, and in all Judea and Samaria, and to the ends of the earth.
>
> —ACTS 1:8

Until he returns, we are commissioned by Jesus to be witnesses. We don't just "do witnessing," but we "are witnesses." The followers in that room with Jesus were witnesses of his resurrection body. Today, we are also witnesses of his resurrected life and power. Ephesians 1:19–20 tells us that the same power that raised Jesus from the dead is in us. When we live lives yielded to the will of God through the power of his indwelling Spirit, we give evidence that God is alive in us.

How we keep our promises, how we treat others, what makes up our priorities, what brings tears to our eyes, where we spend our money, how we engage the poor and the oppressed—all of this gives evidence that Jesus is alive, because we live as he lived in the same strength of the Spirit who empowered him.

Oftentimes people are simply not ready to hear the words of the gospel. Don't force it. Our job is not to be successful but to be faithful as witnesses. The ultimate decision is between them and God. I find that when people experience a crisis, when the "wheels fall off their wagons," when they are confronted with the fragility of life, they are most open to the message of God. In the meantime, just live the message of Jesus' love graciously and winsomely before them. When the time arrives and that tragedy or uncertainty comes into their lives, you will be the person they approach.

Who has God placed in your life right now to be a witness to of the resurrected life of Jesus? I would encourage you to write their names down and keep the list in your Bible or another place where you will see it often. How are you doing in your witness of Jesus to them? A person who truly loves people and believes the message of this book will desperately want to take as many people as possible along with him or her into God's eternal home.

Pray

After John saw the vision of what is to come and how amazing it was, he ended the entire Bible with this prayer: "Come, Lord Jesus" (Revelation 22:20).

For most of my forty-plus-year relationship with Christ, my prayer has not been like John's. It has more honestly been, "I am glad you are coming, Lord, but I would prefer you not come today!" This is the secret prayer of most Christians I know. Why? Well, for me it was because I didn't see the vision as John saw it. I thought the afterlife was all about exiting my body and going up into the heavens as a disembodied spirit, floating in space and singing songs for all eternity.

I sing more than anyone in my family. I almost exclusively sing worship songs. If I am not talking, I am singing. And yet the idea of being a naked spirit, singing 24/7 for all eternity, just falls short of an exciting vision to me. But I think you will agree after our journey together that my early vision of heaven was woefully underinformed. Now that I have a much better understanding of Life Forever on the new earth and my place in the new city with an imperishable body in community with other believers, without the presence of sin and death but with the perpetual presence of God, I find great cause to sing now and throughout eternity. I will even sign up for the choir if one is assembled.

How about you? Where are you on this journey? I have tried my best to be honest with you about my struggles so that you might be encouraged to do the same. Sweeping our fears, doubts, confusion, and anger under the rug is not a healthy solution. Simply getting so busy with life that we don't leave any time to ponder our future is a denial that the end of Life Now is rapidly approaching in light of eternity. It is a clock that can't be stopped. In our journey together we have opened up God's Word to see and understand what he has promised. You have to admit: all that God has in store for those who know him and have received this gift of eternal life is pretty compelling. And you know what? I am quite sure we have only scratched the surface of all that God has planned for us. So enter into the rush of anticipation. As of today, we are one day closer.

Let's commit to joining John and wake up every day praying with passion and anticipation, "Come, Lord Jesus."

Q&A on Life Now

Do we have guardian angels?

The short answer is yes, we do have guardian angels!

The passage of Scripture stating it the clearest is from the teaching of Jesus:

> See that you do not despise one of these little ones. For I tell you that their angels in heaven always see the face of my Father in heaven.
>
> —MATTHEW 18:10

We don't have just one but a collection of them looking out for each believer personally, not just children.

> Are not all angels ministering spirits sent to serve those who will inherit salvation?
>
> —HEBREWS 1:14

Isn't this quite remarkable? When you accepted Jesus for the forgiveness of your sins, God assigned a host of angels to minister to you. This explains at least some of those unexplainable events that just couldn't be coincidental.

133

Are there really enough angels to have several assigned to each believer? The apostle John got a 3-D, IMAX, Dolby surround sound theater vision of the spirit world. At one point the angels were saying aloud in unison, "Worthy is the Lamb, who was slain, to receive power and wealth and wisdom and strength and honor and glory and praise!" (Revelation 5:12). How many were there? John said, "I looked and heard the voice of many angels, numbering thousands upon thousands, and ten thousand times ten thousand" (Revelation 5:11). In Bible interpretation this is known as a rhetorical phrase for an indefinitely large number.

When Jesus was arrested on the night before the crucifixion, one of the disciples grabbed a sword and sliced off the ear of one of the perpetrators. Jesus told him to put away the sword. "Do you think I cannot call on my Father, and he will at once put at my disposal more than twelve legions of angels?" (Matthew 26:53). A Roman legion had six thousand soldiers. Twelve legions would be seventy-two thousand angels just for this one event. I think it is safe to say there are enough angels to cover us all.

Jesus had angels assigned to him when he walked the earth. After Jesus, who was already weak from fasting in the wilderness, denied the devil's three tempting offers, we are told, "the devil left him, and angels came and attended him" (Matthew 4:11).

Our angels can attend to our emotional and spiritual needs when we are exhausted. We see they did the same thing for Jesus in the Garden of Gethsemane. Jesus was experiencing severe anguish at the thought of facing crucifixion the next day. After he prayed, we are told, "an angel from heaven appeared to him and strengthened him" (Luke 22:43). These ministering spirits are on call to do the same for us.

When Daniel was thrown into a den of hungry lions for praying to God, the next morning he reported, "My God sent his angel, and he shut the mouths of the lions" (Daniel 6:22). The lions genuinely wanted a Daniel burger for dinner, but God sent Daniel's guardian angel to shut the lions' mouths.

As I think about it, there have been times in my own life when I think God must have commanded my angels to shut the mouths of several proverbial lions. How about you?

Speaking of lions, Peter tells us:

> Be alert and of sober mind. Your enemy the devil prowls around like a roaring lion looking for someone to devour. Resist him, standing firm in the faith, because you know that the family of believers throughout the world is undergoing the same kind of sufferings.
>
> —1 Peter 5:8–9

We must remember there are two types of angels: those for God and those for Satan. With as much intensity as our angels work to guard us, the devil's angels stalk us like lions, seeking to devour us. We are no match for the devil and his angels. We need our angels to shut their mouths lest we be destroyed.

Paul reminds us that there is more going on in the world than we can see.

> For our struggle is not against flesh and blood, but against the rulers, against the authorities, against the powers of this dark world and against the spiritual forces of evil in the heavenly realms.
>
> —Ephesians 6:12

I think if there were such a thing as a spiritual strobe flashlight that we could shine into the spaces around us, we would see a lot more spirit activity than we ever imagined. Just now, as I was writing this section, I received an e-mail from a friend in Nashville who is scheduled to be here next week to speak powerfully to our large congregation about the persecuted church. His mother-in-law has been hospitalized, so he wanted me to know he may not be able to make it. I cannot be certain, but I feel pretty strongly that the devil and his forces do not want the thousands of believers at our church to get all up in arms about the plight of our brothers and sisters in the Middle East who are being run out of their homes, burned alive, and beheaded. We desperately need the army of God's heavenly host to intervene.

While it is true from Scripture that we have not one but many guardian angels watching over us, there are two things we must remember:

1. God directs them; we do not. We can't tell our assigned angels what to do.

   For he will command his angels concerning you
   to guard you in all your ways.

   —PSALM 91:11

2. We are not to worship angels. We only worship God, the creator of the angels. (Romans 1:25; Colossians 2:18)

Guardian angels are a gift from God, and perhaps their final act in watching over us is revealed in Jesus' parable about the rich man and Lazarus. Jesus said, "The time came when the beggar died and the angels carried him to Abraham's side" (Luke 16:22). When we take our last breath in Life Now and are ushered into Life In Between, how do our spirits get to the presence of God since we have no idea where to go? It is very possible that one or more of our assigned angels will carry us to him. I don't know about you, but I find that very comforting.

Is it okay to be cremated?

It never even occurred to me to ask my mom whether she planned to be buried or cremated. I just assumed she would be buried. Frankly, I didn't know anyone at that time who had been cremated. After my mom's death my dad revealed my mom's wish to be cremated. At first I was quite rattled by the decision. For quite some time I hesitated to tell anyone she had been cremated out of my desire to protect my mom from public scorn or a raised eyebrow. Like my approach with everything else related to the subject of death and the afterlife, I opened the Bible to see what I could find.

At gravesides sometimes you will find the minister throwing dirt onto the sunken casket of the deceased while saying, "Ashes to ashes, dust to dust." This concept comes from Genesis 3 during God's declaration of the curse on humanity for sin:

> By the sweat of your brow
> you will eat your food
> until you return to the ground,
> since from it you were taken;

> for dust you are
> and to dust you will return.
>
> —GENESIS 3:19

Over time, our bodies decay and eventually return to dust and ashes, which is the raw material God made to create us in the first place (Genesis 2:7). Cremation simply expedites the process. Is that right or wrong?

The only passage of the Bible I found that might discourage the practice of cremation is Amos 2:1. Here, God is casting judgment against the people of Moab for their sins:

> This is what the LORD says:
>
> "For three sins of Moab,
>   even for four, I will not relent.
> Because he burned to ashes
>   the bones of Edom's king."

It is important to note that the king of Moab did not kill the king of Edom and then cremate him but actually exhumed the body from the grave and then burned the bones to ashes (the flesh had already decayed). So, in the end, this was not so much an indictment against cremation as it was an indictment against the utterly disrespectful actions of Moab toward the memory of another human being.

As to the argument of God needing our physical bodies intact for the final resurrection, let's walk through that thought a little bit. Throughout history there have been Christians who were burned at the stake for their faith in Christ. Certainly they will not miss out on the resurrection just because their bodies were cremated. In fact, even beyond the persecuted, most people of faith who have died over the centuries are already mere ashes simply from the process of their bodies breaking down.

To look at it from a completely different point of view, I'll point us to what we now know about DNA. In a world where we've seen the basic building blocks of each of us spelled out in our scientific makeup, I think it's pretty clear God doesn't need an actual body to re-create or resurrect us. He has the mathematical formula stored away in his divine files that includes our twenty-three pairs of unique chromosomes that make us who we are. A building that has been burned to the ground can be reconstructed from a good set of blueprints. God has our blueprints.

Also, keep in mind that God is not simply resurrecting our old bodies, but he is giving us new, imperishable bodies (1 Corinthians 15). Some stuff will be taken out of our current bodies and some ingredients will be added to our new bodies. This is all above my pay grade, but the Bible is incredibly clear about this outcome.

In the end, when we're considering what is best to do with our physical bodies after death, the solution boils down to our hearts' intents and attitudes. God certainly wants us to show respect and dignity to our bodies, alive and deceased. If we approach this decision out of sincere reverence for God and prayerful sensitivity to our families, I think God can honor either decision.

It appears the common practice in the Bible, particularly the Old Testament, was burial, but keep in mind that the Bible neither condemns nor condones cremation. If you want to play it safe, go with a burial. As for me, I haven't made my decision yet. I am still holding out for the return of Christ in my lifetime and pray I can avoid the decision altogether!

What about people making predictions about the return of Christ?

Over the centuries numerous people have predicted the return of Christ with great confidence and conviction. To date, all of them have been wrong. So is date setting on Christ's return something we should do or even listen to?

It is a good thing to long for the return of Christ. Remember: John ended the entire Bible with the prayer request, "Come, Lord Jesus" (Revelation 22:20). When we secure and embrace a solid vision of what God has prepared for us for all eternity, we should get super excited about his arrival. However, when asked about his return, Jesus said:

> About that day or hour no one knows, not even the angels in heaven, nor the Son, but only the Father.
>
> —MATTHEW 24:36

When Jesus was walking the earth, he said he didn't even know the date of his return. It is safe to say that if Jesus didn't know, then no man or woman, no matter how religiously savvy or charismatic he or she is, will know for sure.

However, Jesus did tell us there would be signs. Someone has suggested that more than 30 percent of the Bible is made up of prophecies. Some of these prophecies deal with the end of time and the return of

Christ. Because they were given to us, we should understand them and pay attention to them without going so far as to predict an actual date. I think the Bible strongly discourages this kind of conjecture. But if we refrain from going in that direction, we are safe—and even encouraged—to hope and to look for Christ's coming.

Jesus did say in his teaching that we should "keep watch." This means we should live every day with the expectation of his arrival. To be honest, it does seem as if it is taking a long time. I became a Christian back in 1974 at age fourteen. I had never been to church before that time. I was attending a weeklong, summer vacation Bible school event, and the strong theme for the week was, "Accept Christ now before he returns and raptures only believers into heaven." The pastor never said it explicitly, but he did imply, in my opinion, that Jesus was coming back on Friday at the end of vacation Bible school. I accepted Christ on Thursday, just in the nick of time. On Friday I came to the church in a red sport jacket with a country club medallion sewn on the front, ready to be whisked away in the rapture to be with my newfound Savior. But Friday night came and went, and Jesus didn't return. The good news is, since that day I have been ready for when he does come to take us to be with him.

Remember the words of Peter about God's timetable over ours:

> But do not forget this one thing, dear friends: With the Lord a day is like a thousand years, and a thousand years are like a day. The Lord is not slow in keeping his promise, as some understand slowness. Instead he is patient with you, not wanting anyone to perish, but everyone to come to repentance.
>
> —2 Peter 3:8–9

What could possibly be the benefit in God delaying the return of Christ? Peter said that the Lord doesn't want "anyone to perish, but everyone to come to repentance." If Christ came today, that person who would have had the chance to accept Jesus tomorrow would miss out.

In Matthew 24:14, Jesus said, "And this gospel of the kingdom will be preached in the whole world as a testimony to all nations, and then the end will come." Our loving and just God wants to make sure every nation of the world has a chance to hear the offer of life in the kingdom of God before he sends his Son back to us. Some have suggested we are getting very close to achieving this assignment, and it could literally be accomplished in our lifetime.

God came to Abraham in 2091 BC and promised to grow his family of two (including Sarah) into a great nation, and from that nation all nations would be blessed (Genesis 12:1–3). The ultimate blessing would be the arrival of the Messiah through the lineage of Abraham. How long might you have expected it to take God to provide one child from the family of Abraham who would be deemed the Messiah? Because people are people, I am sure they thought it would happen within their lifetime. Well, it took more than two thousand years for Jesus to arrive on the scene. We are just shy of two thousand years since Jesus ascended back to the Father after his resurrection. If it was in the good and sovereign plan of God to take two thousand years for Christ to come the first time, it is not unreasonable to suggest that it is within the good and sovereign plan of God for it to take another two thousand years or more for him to come the second time. I'm not setting any dates; I am simply offering, with my red sport jacket by my side, the advice of Jesus: "Keep watch."

What about life-after-death and near-death experiences?

Life-after-death and near-death experiences fascinate me. Shucks, they fascinate millions of people, if anything can be gleaned from the sales of books and movies on the topic. We so want them to be true. Maybe they are; maybe they aren't. On one end of the spectrum, people cling to these stories to give them the evidence they need that there is more to this life. Others vehemently criticize the experience for a variety of reasons, from medical to theological. As for me, I feel no need to undermine someone's personal experience. However, my commitment and confidence lie within the pages of the Bible. In these pages I find two bona fide life-after-death experiences and two that likely don't qualify but give me tons of hope.

The first involves a guy named Lazarus (John 11). This was not the same man Jesus referred to in the parable with the rich man in Luke 16. This was the brother of Mary and Martha from Bethany. He had been dead a total of not four hours but four days. He was already wrapped in linens and placed in a tomb shut off by a large rock. It is hard to breathe under such circumstances. He was not nearly dead; he was totally dead.

When Jesus finally arrived in Bethany, he had the stone removed from the tomb and commanded Lazarus to rise up and come out. And he did! What did Lazarus say afterward? The text records not a single word. His life-after-death experience is not germane to the point of the story. Rather, Jesus told us the ultimate purpose in a conversation he had with the Father:

> Then Jesus looked up and said, "Father, I thank you that you
> have heard me. I knew that you always hear me, but I said this

for the benefit of the people standing here, that they may believe that you sent me."

—JOHN 11:41–42

In the end, the most important thing is that all would be pointed to belief in Jesus. Our focus should not be the life-after-death or near-death experience but the more important, personal experience with and belief in the One who saves.

I can imagine Lazarus saying privately to Jesus, "I was at Abraham's side with the other Lazarus guy you taught about. It was very restful and peaceful. I just have one question: Do I have to go through death again?" The answer would most definitely have been yes. Lazarus was brought back to life, only to have to eventually experience death once again. What a bummer, in my book.

The second life-after-death experience in the Bible is that of Jesus himself. He died and lay in the tomb for three days. On Sunday morning he rose from the dead. He went on to appear in front of hundreds of people. His return to life was very different from Lazarus's. Jesus was resurrected once and for all. He conquered death; he didn't have to die again.

Over the years, people have read about this event. Many have believed it, and many have rejected it. You may doubt the veracity of near-death experiences, but this life-after-death experience is the only one that really matters. Your personal decision about this experience will be the sole determining factor in the outcome of your own eventual eternal destination.

The next story we find in the Bible carries a similar theme and tone to the modern-day near-death experiences we read about. It is the true story of Stephen, the first martyr of the church.

Stephen, having been seized in Jerusalem by people opposing the early church, gave a stirring speech that he concluded by identifying his hostile audience as the perpetrators who had killed the Messiah. This infuriated them. They decide to stone him to death. At the moment of their decision, while Stephen was still alive, something happened to him that was out of the ordinary:

> Stephen, full of the Holy Spirit, looked up to heaven and saw the glory of God, and Jesus standing at the right hand of God. "Look," he said, "I see heaven open and the Son of Man standing at the right hand of God."
>
> —ACTS 7:55–56

This encounter is similar to the stories we hear from Christians in modern near-death experiences. They see a light; they see the glory of God; they see Jesus. It is interesting to note that in other passages of Scripture where Jesus is in heaven next to the Father, he is sitting. In this case, Jesus was standing. It is as if he were telling Stephen, "You have stood up for me on earth; now I am standing up for you in heaven. Keep your eyes fixed on me. Everything is going to be all right. You will be in my presence very soon."

After this, the mob took Stephen outside the city and stoned him to death. His body died, but his spirit went to be in the presence of Jesus. This glimpse into Stephen's vision gives us hope as we face our own valleys of death.

Paul had a similar experience, though it was not centered on his death but on his stoning at Lystra. He wrote:

I know a man in Christ who fourteen years ago was caught up to the third heaven. Whether it was in the body or out of the body I do not know—God knows. And I know that this man—whether in the body or apart from the body I do not know, but God knows—was caught up to paradise and heard inexpressible things.

—2 CORINTHIANS 12:2–4

Paul told us he saw the "third heaven," or "paradise." The third heaven designates a place beyond the earth's atmosphere and beyond the planets and stars to the presence of God himself. Paul reaffirmed the existence of this higher plane in his later letter to the Ephesian believers: "He who descended is the very one who ascended higher than all the heavens, in order to fill the whole universe" (4:10).

This is confirmation that the dwelling place of believers in the intermediate state is beyond our universe. That is helpful to know. What else did Paul see while in the third heaven? We actually don't know, because he went on to tell us that the things he saw "no one is permitted to tell." Interestingly, people with life-after-death and near-death experiences today freely share what they saw, but Paul felt it was not permissible for anyone to do so.

As we consider the ramifications of all our modern-day sharing of life-after-death and near-death experiences, we must go back to Jesus' teaching and the story of the rich man and Lazarus. When the rich man begged Abraham to let Lazarus return to earth to warn his brothers of Hades, remember that Abraham replied:

They have Moses and the Prophets; let them listen to them. . . . If they do not listen to Moses and the Prophets, they will not be convinced even if someone rises from the dead.

—LUKE 16:29, 31

Life-after-death and near-death experiences are very intriguing, at least to me. If they inspire us to draw closer to God and increase our hope in the afterlife, then great. But at the end of the day, we must be able to stand on the truth that the Word of God is enough. As Abraham said in the story above, we have the teachings of Moses and the prophets to point us to God, but even further, believers today also have twenty-seven New Testament books filled with new revelation. We have been given a wealth of wisdom and insight that is enough to lead us to Jesus.

My favorite heavenly vision of all is found in Revelation 21–22. And because it is in God's Word, I can say with confidence, "Heaven is for real."

A Word from the Author

Prayer Wall

THE CITY OF JERUSALEM IS THE HOME OF THE FAMOUS Wailing Wall. Jews come to this wall daily to pray for the coming of the Messiah, the One who will save them from their sins and restore that relationship with God. We Christians celebrate that the Messiah has already come. His name is Jesus. He has made the way for all people to come into an eternal relationship with God.

We now go to our own "Wailing Wall" to pray for people to believe in the Messiah and to receive this gift of eternal life. Perhaps you have someone in your life who hasn't received Christ. Maybe it's a spouse or one of your children, a neighbor, a coworker, or a friend. Maybe you need to place your own name on the wall. I invite you to go to http://prayer.randyfrazee.com/ and place the name of this person or persons on this virtual wall so that others can pray with you. You can use a name or initials, include the state or country where the person lives, and leave a short note or prayer. We have a team of committed prayer warriors who will be faithful to pray for the person you place on the wall. Please join in and take time to pray for the name of someone else on this wall. God is listening.

Discussion Questions for Small Groups

INTRODUCTION: WHAT'S NEXT?

1. Do you fear death?
2. If you have lost someone close to you, share that experience and how it has affected your faith.
3. On page xv, we read that at the beginning of his journey, Randy confessed, "I don't believe in heaven." Where are you in terms of your belief in and excitement about heaven?
4. How have movies, television programs, popular literature, and songs shaped your thinking about the afterlife? (See page xvi.)
5. First Corinthians 2:10 tells us God has revealed what he has prepared for those who love him. What is the biggest question you most long to have answered in this study?

CHAPTER 1: IS JESUS ENOUGH?

1. On page 1, Randy says, "Could salvation really be as simple as receiving a gift, particularly a gift you do not deserve? . . .

151

No other area of life gives so much and requires so little from the recipient." What do you think?

2. On pages 2–3, Randy refers to different steps various Christian denominations lay out to receive salvation and eternal life. What background do you come from, if any, and what are the steps that group asks you to take?

3. Do you agree with Randy's interpretation on page 5 that reconciles Jesus' conversation with the rich young ruler and his other teachings?

4. Do you think there is a big difference between understanding the steps of salvation and believing them in your heart? (See page 10.) Do you think this makes any difference in the outcome of one's salvation?

5. Would you say you have personally believed in Jesus in your heart and publicly confessed this decision to others? If yes, share your experience. If not, what is holding you back?

CHAPTER 2: WHAT HAPPENS IF I DIE WITHOUT CHRIST?

1. On page 21, Randy wrote, "The Old Testament has very little to say about the afterlife, or what we're calling 'Life In Between,' and the New Testament only has a few verses about this second stage." Why do you think this is the case?

2. If a person reads Luke 16 or this chapter, how can he or she still reject Christ? What do you think still holds people back even when they have been exposed to this teaching?

3. What do you think of the sentence on page 27, "God doesn't send anyone to hell; he merely honors a person's choice"?
4. The rich man in Luke 16 begged Abraham to send Lazarus back to warn his brothers of Hades. Why did Abraham say this wouldn't work to convince them? (See page 28.)
5. Do you have someone in your life right now who has openly rejected or simply ignores the message of this chapter? Share his or her name with the group. Consider adding that person's name to the prayer wall to engage others in praying for your loved one. (See page 149.)

CHAPTER 3: WHAT HAPPENS IF I DIE WITH CHRIST?

1. Randy suggests that part of the fear of dying comes from never having experienced it before. What do you think? (See page 32.)
2. On page 37, Randy concludes that after Jesus' death but before his resurrection, he went to Abraham's side to retrieve the spirits whose bodies had died before Christ's death and took them directly into the presence of God. Why did Jesus do this? What do you think this encounter was like for those who experienced it?
3. In 2 Corinthians 5:8 Paul said he would rather "be away from the body and at home with the Lord." Can you honestly say that? Why or why not?

4. What was Paul's secret to getting to the place where he was excited about being in Life In Between? (See pages 39–46.)

5. If you are a believer in Jesus, what excites you the most about being in heaven?

Q&A ON LIFE IN BETWEEN

1. How do you feel about living in Life In Between without being contained in a body?

2. If someone told you he saw a ghost, what would you say to him? (See page 50.)

3. In what ways would having our loved ones looking down on us from heaven be a good thing and a bad thing? (See page 53.)

4. Christ paid for all our sins. Do you believe we receive total forgiveness for all our sins, past, present, and future, when we first trust Christ, or that we need to continually approach God to receive that forgiveness? (See page 54.)

5. Even though the Bible doesn't explicitly teach there are different degrees of hell, it doesn't mean there are not. Do you think there should be various degrees of punishment based on the way a nonbeliever lived his or her life on earth? (See page 56.)

CHAPTER 4: WHAT HAPPENS IF I DON'T KNOW CHRIST WHEN HE RETURNS?

1. Why is everyone who stands before the Great White Throne of judgment declared guilty? (See page 58.)

2. Have you ever been to the funeral of a person who clearly did not trust or follow Christ in his or her lifetime but the minister led you to believe that person was in heaven? In what ways is this a good thing? In what ways is this dangerous?

3. How many sins does a person have to commit to make him or her guilty and be declared condemned? (See James 2:10 and page 69.) Why is the bar set so high?

4. On page 69, Randy says that people being thrown into the lake of fire is "the only thing a righteous, just, and loving God can do." Do you agree? Why or why not?

5. After reading pages 70–73, do you agree with the position of "eternal punishment" or "eternal punishing"? Why?

CHAPTER 5: WHAT HAPPENS IF I DO KNOW CHRIST WHEN HE RETURNS?

1. Has the death of someone you love ever rattled your faith? If so, how?

2. Is the fact that our eternal dwelling place is not *up in heaven* but *down on a new earth* a new discovery for you? What do you think of this? (See page 83.)

3. What do you think it's going to be like to actually meet God—Father, Son, and Holy Spirit? (See pages 82–83.)

4. What are you looking forward to the most about your new, imperishable body? (See pages 104–109.)

5. What intrigues you the most about the New Jerusalem? (See pages 110–112.)

Q&A ON LIFE FOREVER

1. Given that the Bible clearly states there will be rewards in the new kingdom (pages 93–96), what would you change in your Life Now to build your divine 401(k)? What do you think constitutes wood, hay, stubble, gold, silver, and precious stones?

2. With the idea that all manner of creatures in the new kingdom will get along, what kind of pet would you want to have? (See pages 97–99.) Would you like to stay with a cat or dog, or have as a pet an animal that was more dangerous and untouchable on the old earth? If so, which one?

3. Randy says on page 99, "As Jesus' index finger swipes across our cheeks, I believe the memories of our previous life on the old earth will be gone." Ponder what you think this means and what it doesn't mean.

4. What do you think of there being no marriage or giving of marriage in the new kingdom? (See pages 101–102.)

5. Randy stated on page 109 that he thinks we will be on a vegetarian diet in the new kingdom, as Adam and Eve were in the original garden. Why is this important, and how do you feel about it?

6. Share some of the activities you hope will still be available in the new kingdom that you perhaps don't have enough time for here in Life Now. (See page 112.) Do you think your job or career will be needed in the new kingdom? (See page 110.)

CHAPTER 6: UNTIL THEN

1. Share a story from your life that demonstrates the power of anticipation.
2. Why does Scripture encourage us to "live holy and godly lives" now as we anticipate our future life with God? Give one example of what living such a life looks like today. (See page 118.)
3. How does the truth about the afterlife enable us to live without fear today? What is one practical thing we can do to lower our level of fear in this life? (See page 121.)
4. Identify one person who could be encouraged by what you have learned from this book. What is the best way to offer such encouragement (a phone call, a text, forwarding a song, sending a handwritten note)? Go ahead and do it! (See page 127.)
5. Who is someone you know personally who has not accepted Christ? What is one thing you can do to be a positive witness of Christ to him or her? (See page 129.)
6. After reading this book are you more eager to pray the prayer of John, "Come, Lord Jesus"? Why or why not?

Q&A ON LIFE NOW

1. How do you feel about having a collection of angels assigned to you personally? Has there been a time in your life when

you might have sensed their presence or involvement in your life? (See page 133.)

2. Do you personally think being cremated is okay? Have you made a decision about your body yet? (See pages 137–140.)

3. Even though we should not make predictions on the exact return of Christ, do you think Christ will return in your lifetime? Why or why not? (See page 140.)

4. What do you think about life-after-death and near-death experiences? How do you determine what is actually true? (See page 143.)

5. What is the one question you would like to ask God the first time you meet him?

Acknowledgments

I WANT TO THANK MY BEST FRIEND AND WIFE OF thirty-five years. We started sitting together in church when I was fifteen and only a year old in my faith. Every personal story you read about in the book from age fifteen on, Rozanne has been by my side, experiencing it with me, believing in me, consoling me, forgiving me, and rooting for me. She has read and edited all my books and in every case has made them much better. We have even written two together. Rozanne, looks like I won't be your husband on the new earth, but I still plan to be your best friend. Until then, I will cherish every day we have left as husband and wife.

Our four children, Jennifer, David, Stephen, and Austin, have been the biggest motivators in my life. I don't want to be a dad who just talks about stuff; I want to trust God enough in my life to live it out in front of them so they may know the way. On days I have been willing to settle for less, I look at my grown kids, their spouses (Desmond and Gretchen), and now my first two grandchildren (Ava and Crew Rand), and step it up. Legacy matters to me. More often than not these days, the table has been turned, and they are the ones who are inspiring me. I am so proud of you guys.

Rozanne's favorite section in this book is the question I answer about guardian angels. Well, my guardian angel just might be Nancy Zack, my assistant now for more than a decade. She not only helps me with every book I write, but she helps run every area of my life. She thinks for me. She saves me from follies and foibles. She has honed her craft to perfection. Nancy, if a human being could earn wings, you most definitely would have earned a pair just for watching over me.

Gratitude abounds for Max Lucado, my teaching partner at Oak Hills Church. What a joy it has been to serve next to one of the most prolific, effective, and heartfelt writers of our generation. Max's words inspire me, but the life he lives inspires me more. Standing right next to Max and me is the wonderful staff of Oak Hills, led by Mark Tidwell. They bring their "A-game" every day to serve the city of San Antonio and beyond. Together with God's help and strength, we are partnering to increase the population of heaven.

I have never written a book without acknowledging Mike Reilly and Bob Buford. Both men, for reasons beyond me, have come alongside me since my twenties and have faithfully blown wind in my sails. Their support has enabled me to overcome large waves, get through difficult storms, and cover a lot of nautical miles for the kingdom. Thank you, thank you.

There's cause for rejoicing for my team at Nelson Books. They are the best of the best. Making books is a business for most. For them it is a ministry; it is all about impact in people's lives that revs their engines. Jessica Wong, Janene MacIvor, and Renee Chavez, my editors, have been just delightful. They combed over every chapter, every paragraph, and every word with the desire to make it the best it can be for you, the reader. Authors are tender folks with a great deal of pride for the message they believe in so strongly. These books are our babies. Most parents don't like advice from others on how to raise their babies. Jessica, Janene, and Renee, in their Christlike demeanor, were able to come alongside me with grace and blew me away by their sheer intelligence and excellence. They are keepers.

Who could ever tire of thanking God? I don't do it haphazardly. Without Jesus Christ nothing in this book would be true. He has proven himself to be trustworthy by keeping every single one of the promises he has made so far. I am hanging all my hope on the confidence he will follow through on this final promise of eternal life with him in the new kingdom. I have no plan B. Don't need one.

Randy Frazee
San Antonio, Texas

Scriptures

INTRODUCTION

You will know the truth, and the truth will set you free.

—JOHN 8:32

It is written:

> "What no eye has seen,
>   what no ear has heard,
> and what no human mind has conceived"—
>   the things God has prepared for those who love him—
> these are the things God has revealed to us by his Spirit.

—1 CORINTHIANS 2:9–10

CHAPTER 1: IS JESUS ENOUGH?

As the body without the spirit is dead, so faith without deeds is dead.

—JAMES 2:26

163

Salvation is found in no one else, for there is no other name under heaven given to mankind by which we must be saved.

—ACTS 4:12

As Jesus started on his way, a man ran up to him and fell on his knees before him. "Good teacher," he asked, "what must I do to inherit eternal life?"

"Why do you call me good?" Jesus answered. "No one is good—except God alone. You know the commandments: 'You shall not murder, you shall not commit adultery, you shall not steal, you shall not give false testimony, you shall not defraud, honor your father and mother.'"

"Teacher," he declared, "all these I have kept since I was a boy."

Jesus looked at him and loved him. "One thing you lack," he said. "Go, sell everything you have and give to the poor, and you will have treasure in heaven. Then come, follow me."

At this the man's face fell. He went away sad, because he had great wealth.

—MARK 10:17–22

For it is by grace you have been saved, through faith—and this is not from yourselves, it is the gift of God—not by works, so that no one can boast.

—EPHESIANS 2:8–9

For God so loved the world that he gave his one and only Son, that whoever believes in him shall not perish but have eternal life.

—JOHN 3:16

Whoever believes in the Son has eternal life, but whoever rejects the Son will not see life, for God's wrath remains on them.

—JOHN 3:36

Very truly I tell you, whoever hears my word and believes him who sent me has eternal life and will not be judged but has crossed over from death to life.

—JOHN 5:24

For my Father's will is that everyone who looks to the Son and believes in him shall have eternal life, and I will raise them up at the last day.

—JOHN 6:40

Very truly I tell you, the one who believes has eternal life.

—JOHN 6:47

If you declare with your mouth, "Jesus is Lord," and believe in your heart that God raised him from the dead, you will be saved. For it is with your heart that you believe and are justified, and it is with your mouth that you profess your faith and are saved.

—ROMANS 10:9–10

What good is it for someone to gain the whole world, and yet lose or forfeit their very self? Whoever is ashamed of me and my words, the Son of Man will be ashamed of them when he comes in his glory and in the glory of the Father and of the holy angels.

—LUKE 9:25–26

"Therefore let all Israel be assured of this: God has made this Jesus, whom you crucified, both Lord and Messiah."

When the people heard this, they were cut to the heart and said to Peter and the other apostles, "Brothers, what shall we do?"

Peter replied, "Repent and be baptized, every one of you, in the name of Jesus Christ for the forgiveness of your sins. And you will receive the gift of the Holy Spirit. The promise is for you and your children and for all who are far off—for all whom the Lord our God will call."

—ACTS 2:36–39

We all, like sheep, have gone astray,
> each of us has turned to our own way;
and the LORD has laid on him
> the iniquity of us all.

—ISAIAH 53:6

You study the Scriptures diligently because you think that in them you have eternal life. These are the very Scriptures that testify about me, yet you refuse to come to me to have life.

—JOHN 5:39–40

CHAPTER 2: WHAT HAPPENS IF I DIE WITHOUT CHRIST?

Altogether, Methuselah lived a total of 969 years, and then he died.

—GENESIS 5:27

There was a rich man who was dressed in purple and fine linen and lived in luxury every day. At his gate was laid a beggar named Lazarus, covered with sores and longing to eat what fell from the rich man's table. Even the dogs came and licked his sores.

The time came when the beggar died and the angels carried him to Abraham's side. The rich man also died and was buried. In Hades, where he was in torment, he looked up and saw Abraham far away, with Lazarus by his side. So he called to him, "Father Abraham, have pity on me and send Lazarus to dip the tip of his finger in water and cool my tongue, because I am in agony in this fire."

But Abraham replied, "Son, remember that in your lifetime you received your good things, while Lazarus received bad things, but now he is comforted here and you are in agony. And besides all this, between us and you a great chasm has been set in place, so that those who want to go from here to you cannot, nor can anyone cross over from there to us."

—LUKE 16:19–26

We all, like sheep, have gone astray,
    each of us has turned to our own way;
and the LORD has laid on him
    the iniquity of us all.

—ISAIAH 53:6

Then he will say to those on his left, "Depart from me, you who are cursed, into the eternal fire prepared for the devil and his angels."

—MATTHEW 25:41

They are wild waves of the sea, foaming up their shame; wandering stars, for whom blackest darkness has been reserved forever.

—JUDE 13

They will suffer the punishment of eternal destruction, away from the presence of the Lord and from the glory of his might.

—THESSALONIANS 1:9

So the LORD God banished him from the Garden of Eden to work the ground from which he had been taken. After he drove the man out, he placed on the east side of the Garden of Eden cherubim and a flaming sword flashing back and forth to guard the way to the tree of life.

—GENESIS 3:23–24

He answered, "Then I beg you, father, send Lazarus to my family, for I have five brothers. Let him warn them, so that they will not also come to this place of torment."

Abraham replied, "They have Moses and the Prophets; let them listen to them."

"No, father Abraham," he said, "but if someone from the dead goes to them, they will repent."

He said to him, "If they do not listen to Moses and the Prophets, they will not be convinced even if someone rises from the dead."

—LUKE 16:27–31

It is appointed unto men once to die, but after this the judgment.

—HEBREWS 9:27 KJV

CHAPTER 3: WHAT HAPPENS IF I DIE WITH CHRIST?

So the LORD God banished him from the Garden of Eden to work the ground from which he had been taken. After he drove the man out, he placed on the east side of the Garden of Eden cherubim and a flaming sword flashing back and forth to guard the way to the tree of life.

—GENESIS 3:23–24

"This is to be a lasting ordinance for you: Atonement is to be made once a year for all the sins of the Israelites."

And it was done, as the LORD commanded Moses.

—LEVITICUS 16:34

The law is only a shadow of the good things that are coming— not the realities themselves. For this reason it can never, by the same sacrifices repeated endlessly year after year, make perfect those who draw near to worship. Otherwise, would they not have stopped being offered? For the worshipers would have been cleansed once for all, and would no longer have felt guilty for their sins. But those sacrifices are an annual reminder of sins. It is impossible for the blood of bulls and goats to take away sins.

—HEBREWS 10:1–4

The next day John saw Jesus coming toward him and said, "Look, the Lamb of God, who takes away the sin of the world!"

—JOHN 1:29

Therefore, when Christ came into the world, he said:

> "Sacrifice and offering you did not desire,
>   but a body you prepared for me;
> with burnt offerings and sin offerings
>   you were not pleased.
> Then I said, 'Here I am—it is written about me in the
>   scroll—
>   I have come to do your will, my God.'"

First he said, "Sacrifices and offerings, burnt offerings and sin offerings you did not desire, nor were you pleased with them"— though they were offered in accordance with the law. Then he said, "Here I am, I have come to do your will." He sets aside the first to establish the second. And by that will, we have been made holy through the sacrifice of the body of Jesus Christ once for all.

—HEBREWS 10:5–10

Jesus answered him, "Truly I tell you, today you will be with me in paradise."

—LUKE 23:43

Whoever has ears, let them hear what the Spirit says to the churches. To the one who is victorious, I will give the right to eat from the tree of life, which is in the paradise of God.

—REVELATION 2:7

Because we know that the one who raised the Lord Jesus from the dead will also raise us with Jesus and present us with you to himself.

—2 CORINTHIANS 4:14

If you declare with your mouth, "Jesus is Lord," and believe in your heart that God raised him from the dead, you will be saved.

—ROMANS 10:9

Therefore we do not lose heart. Though outwardly we are wasting away, yet inwardly we are being renewed day by day. For our light and momentary troubles are achieving for us an eternal glory that far outweighs them all. So we fix our eyes not on what is seen, but on what is unseen, since what is seen is temporary, but what is unseen is eternal. For we know that if the earthly tent we live in is destroyed, we have a building from God, an eternal house in heaven, not built by human hands.

—2 CORINTHIANS 4:16–5:1

Meanwhile we groan, longing to be clothed instead with our heavenly dwelling, because when we are clothed, we will not be found naked. For while we are in this tent, we groan and are burdened, because we do not wish to be unclothed but to be clothed instead with our heavenly dwelling, so that what is mortal may be swallowed up by life. Now the one who has fashioned us for this very purpose is God, who has given us the Spirit as a deposit, guaranteeing what is to come.

—2 CORINTHIANS 5:2–5

Therefore we are always confident and know that as long as we are at home in the body we are away from the Lord. For we live by faith, not by sight. We are confident, I say, and would prefer to be away from the body and at home with the Lord.

—2 CORINTHIANS 5:6–8

For to me, to live is Christ and to die is gain. If I am to go on living in the body, this will mean fruitful labor for me. Yet what shall I choose? I do not know! I am torn between the two: I desire to depart and be with Christ, which is better by far.

—PHILIPPIANS 1:21–23

What is more, I consider everything a loss because of the surpassing worth of knowing Christ Jesus my Lord, for whose sake I have lost all things. I consider them garbage, that I may gain Christ.

—PHILIPPIANS 3:8

Q&A ON LIFE IN BETWEEN

Brothers and sisters, we do not want you to be uninformed about those who sleep in death, so that you do not grieve like the rest of mankind, who have no hope.

—1 THESSALONIANS 4:13

He said to them, "Why are you troubled, and why do doubts rise in your minds? Look at my hands and my feet. It is I myself! Touch me and see; a ghost does not have flesh and bones, as you see I have."

—LUKE 24:38–39

The king said to her, "Don't be afraid. What do you see?"

The woman said, "I see a ghostly figure coming up out of the earth."

"What does he look like?" he asked.

"An old man wearing a robe is coming up," she said.

Then Saul knew it was Samuel, and he bowed down and prostrated himself with his face to the ground.

Samuel said to Saul, "Why have you disturbed me by bringing me up?"

"I am in great distress," Saul said. "The Philistines are fighting against me, and God has departed from me. He no longer answers me, either by prophets or by dreams. So I have called on you to tell me what to do."

—1 SAMUEL 28:13–15

Do not turn to mediums or seek out spiritists, for you will be defiled by them. I am the LORD your God.

—LEVITICUS 19:31

When someone tells you to consult mediums and spiritists, who whisper and mutter, should not a people inquire of their God? Why consult the dead on behalf of the living?

—ISAIAH 8:19

But if he was looking to the splendid reward that is laid up for those who fall asleep in godliness, it was a holy and pious thought. Therefore he made atonement for the dead, so that they might be delivered from their sin.

—2 MACCABEES 12:45 NRSVA

But now he has reconciled you by Christ's physical body through death to present you holy in his sight, without blemish and free from accusation.

—COLOSSIANS 1:22

Jesus answered, "You would have no power over me if it were not given to you from above. Therefore the one who handed me over to you is guilty of a greater sin."

—JOHN 19:11

Anyone who rejected the law of Moses died without mercy on the testimony of two or three witnesses. How much more severely do you think someone deserves to be punished who has trampled the Son of God underfoot, who has treated as an unholy thing the blood of the covenant that sanctified them, and who has insulted the Spirit of grace?

—HEBREWS 10:28–29

In the year that King Uzziah died, I saw the Lord, high and exalted, seated on a throne; and the train of his robe filled the temple.

—ISAIAH 6:1

CHAPTER 4: WHAT HAPPENS IF I DON'T KNOW CHRIST WHEN HE RETURNS?

I saw heaven standing open and there before me was a white horse, whose rider is called Faithful and True. With justice he judges and wages war. His eyes are like blazing fire, and on his head are many crowns. He has a name written on him that no one knows but he himself. He is dressed in a robe dipped in blood, and his name is the Word of God. The armies of heaven were following him, riding on white horses and dressed in fine linen, white and clean. Coming out of his mouth is a sharp sword with which to strike down the nations. "He will rule them with an iron scepter." He treads the winepress of the fury of the wrath of God Almighty. On his robe and on his thigh he has this name written:

KING OF KINGS AND LORD OF LORDS.

—REVELATION 19:11–16

The great dragon was hurled down—that ancient serpent called the devil, or Satan, who leads the whole world astray. He was hurled to the earth, and his angels with him. . . . He seized the dragon, that ancient serpent, who is the devil, or Satan, and bound him for a thousand years.

—REVELATION 12:9; 20:2

Then I saw a great white throne and him who was seated on it. The earth and the heavens fled from his presence, and there was no place for them.

—REVELATION 20:11

And I saw the dead, great and small, standing before the throne, and books were opened. Another book was opened, which is the book of life. The dead were judged according to what they had done as recorded in the books. The sea gave up the dead that were in it, and death and Hades gave up the dead that were in them, and each person was judged according to what they had done.

—REVELATION 20:12–13

Very truly I tell you, whoever hears my word and believes him who sent me has eternal life and will not be judged but has crossed over from death to life.

—JOHN 5:24

Therefore, there is now no condemnation for those who are in Christ Jesus. . . . Who will bring any charge against those whom God has chosen? It is God who justifies. Who then is the one who condemns? No one. Christ Jesus who died—more than that, who was raised to life—is at the right hand of God and is also interceding for us.

—ROMANS 8:1, 33–34

Then death and Hades were thrown into the lake of fire. The lake of fire is the second death. Anyone whose name was not found written in the book of life was thrown into the lake of fire.

—REVELATION 20:14–15

And the devil, who deceived them, was thrown into the lake of burning sulfur, where the beast and the false prophet had been thrown. They will be tormented day and night for ever and ever.

—REVELATION 20:10

Do not be afraid of those who kill the body but cannot kill the soul. Rather, be afraid of the One who can destroy both soul and body in hell.

—MATTHEW 10:28

But the cowardly, the unbelieving, the vile, the murderers, the sexually immoral, those who practice magic arts, the idolaters and all liars—they will be consigned to the fiery lake of burning sulfur. This is the second death.

—REVELATION 21:8

CHAPTER 5: WHAT HAPPENS IF I DO KNOW CHRIST WHEN HE RETURNS?

It is written:

"What no eye has seen,
what no ear has heard,
and what no human mind has conceived"—
the things God has prepared for those who love him—
these are the things God has revealed to us by his Spirit.

—I CORINTHIANS 2:9–10

While we wait for the blessed hope—the appearing of the glory of our great God and Savior, Jesus Christ.

—TITUS 2:13

But Christ has indeed been raised from the dead, the firstfruits of those who have fallen asleep. For since death came through a man, the resurrection of the dead comes also through a man. For as in Adam all die, so in Christ all will be made alive. . . . I declare to you, brothers and sisters, that flesh and blood cannot inherit the kingdom of God, nor does the perishable inherit the imperishable. Listen, I tell you a mystery: We will not all sleep, but we will all be changed—in a flash, in the twinkling of an eye, at the last trumpet. For the trumpet will sound, the dead will be raised imperishable, and we will be changed. For the perishable must clothe itself with the imperishable, and the mortal with immortality. When the perishable has been clothed with the imperishable, and the mortal with immortality, then the saying that is written will come true: "Death has been swallowed up in victory."

—1 CORINTHIANS 20–22, 50–54

And I heard a loud voice from the throne saying, "Look! God's dwelling place is now among the people, and he will dwell with them. They will be his people, and God himself will be with them and be their God."

—REVELATION 21:3

Then I saw "a new heaven and a new earth," for the first heaven and the first earth had passed away, and there was no longer any sea. I saw the Holy City, the new Jerusalem, coming down out of heaven from God, prepared as a bride beautifully dressed for her husband. And I heard a loud voice from the throne saying, "Look! God's dwelling place is now among the people, and he will dwell with them. They will be his people, and God himself will be with them and be their God. 'He will wipe every tear from their eyes. There will be no more death' or mourning or crying or pain, for the old order of things has passed away."

He who was seated on the throne said, "I am making everything new!"

—REVELATION 21:1–5

The angel who talked with me had a measuring rod of gold to measure the city, its gates and its walls. The city was laid out like a square, as long as it was wide. He measured the city with the rod and found it to be 12,000 stadia in length, and as wide and high as it is long. The angel measured the wall using human measurement, and it was 144 cubits thick.

—REVELATION 21:15–17

Do not let your hearts be troubled. You believe in God; believe also in me. My Father's house has many rooms; if that were not so, would I have told you that I am going there to prepare a place for you? And if I go and prepare a place for you, I will come back and take you to be with me that you also may be where I am.

—JOHN 14:1–3

Let not your heart be troubled: ye believe in God, believe also in me. In my Father's house are many mansions: if it were not so, I would have told you. I go to prepare a place for you. And if I go and prepare a place for you, I will come again, and receive you unto myself; that where I am, there ye may be also.

—JOHN 14:1–3 KJV

The wall was made of jasper, and the city of pure gold, as pure as glass. The foundations of the city walls were decorated with every kind of precious stone. The first foundation was jasper, the second sapphire, the third agate, the fourth emerald, the fifth onyx, the sixth ruby, the seventh chrysolite, the eighth beryl, the ninth topaz, the tenth turquoise, the eleventh jacinth, and the twelfth amethyst. The twelve gates were twelve pearls, each gate made of a single pearl. The great street of the city was of gold, as pure as transparent glass.

—REVELATION 21:18–21

I did not see a temple in the city, because the Lord God Almighty and the Lamb are its temple. The city does not need the sun or the moon to shine on it, for the glory of God gives it light, and the Lamb is its lamp. The nations will walk by its light, and the kings of the earth will bring their splendor into it. On no day will its gates ever be shut, for there will be no night there. The glory and honor of the nations will be brought into it. Nothing impure will ever enter it, nor will anyone who does what is shameful or deceitful, but only those whose names are written in the Lamb's book of life.

—REVELATION 21:22–27

Then the angel showed me the river of the water of life, as clear as crystal, flowing from the throne of God and of the Lamb down the middle of the great street of the city. On each side of the river stood the tree of life, bearing twelve crops of fruit, yielding its fruit every month. And the leaves of the tree are for the healing of the nations. No longer will there be any curse. The throne of God and of the Lamb will be in the city, and his servants will serve him. They will see his face, and his name will be on their foreheads. There will be no more night. They will not need the light of a lamp or the light of the sun, for the Lord God will give them light. And they will reign for ever and ever.

—REVELATION 22:1–5

Q&A ON LIFE FOREVER

For we must all appear before the judgment seat of Christ, so that each of us may receive what is due us for the things done while in the body, whether good or bad.

—2 CORINTHIANS 5:10

The one who plants and the one who waters have one purpose, and they will each be rewarded according to their own labor. . . . For no one can lay any foundation other than the one already laid, which is Jesus Christ. If anyone builds on this foundation using gold, silver, costly stones, wood, hay or straw, their work will be shown for what it is, because the Day will bring it to light. It will be revealed with fire, and the fire will test the quality of each person's work. If what has been built survives, the builder will receive a reward. If it is burned up, the builder will suffer loss but yet will be saved—even though only as one escaping through the flames.

—1 CORINTHIANS 3:8, 11–15

The Son of Man is going to come in his Father's glory with his angels, and then he will reward each person according to what they have done.

—MATTHEW 16:27

Religion that God our Father accepts as pure and faultless is this: to look after orphans and widows in their distress and to keep oneself from being polluted by the world.

—JAMES 1:27

You will be blessed. Although they cannot repay you, you will be repaid at the resurrection of the righteous.

—LUKE 14:14

But I tell you that everyone will have to give account on the day of judgment for every empty word they have spoken.

—MATTHEW 12:36

Therefore judge nothing before the appointed time; wait until the Lord comes. He will bring to light what is hidden in darkness and will expose the motives of the heart. At that time each will receive their praise from God.

—1 CORINTHIANS 4:5

My conscience is clear, but that does not make me innocent. It is the Lord who judges me.

—1 CORINTHIANS 4:4

Do not store up for yourselves treasures on earth, where moths and vermin destroy, and where thieves break in and steal. But store up for yourselves treasures in heaven, where moths and vermin do not destroy, and where thieves do not break in and steal.

—MATTHEW 6:19–20

And God said, "Let the water teem with living creatures, and let birds fly above the earth across the vault of the sky." So God created the great creatures of the sea and every living thing with which the water teems and that moves about in it, according to their kinds, and every winged bird according to its kind. And God saw that it was good. God blessed them and said, "Be fruitful and increase in number and fill the water in the seas, and let the birds increase on the earth."

—GENESIS 1:20–22

And God said, "Let the land produce living creatures according to their kinds: the livestock, the creatures that move along the ground, and the wild animals, each according to its kind." And it was so. God made the wild animals according to their kinds, the livestock according to their kinds, and all the creatures that move along the ground according to their kinds. And God saw that it was good.

—GENESIS 1:24–25

"The wolf and the lamb will feed together,
and the lion will eat straw like the ox,
and dust will be the serpent's food.
They will neither harm nor destroy
on all my holy mountain,"
says the LORD.

—ISAIAH 65:25

The wolf will live with the lamb,
the leopard will lie down with the goat,
the calf and the lion and the yearling together;
and a little child will lead them.

—ISAIAH 11:6

"He will wipe every tear from their eyes. There will be no more death" or mourning or crying or pain, for the old order of things has passed away.

—REVELATION 21:4

See, I will create
>   new heavens and a new earth.
The former things will not be remembered,
>   nor will they come to mind.
But be glad and rejoice forever
>   in what I will create,
for I will create Jerusalem to be a delight
>   and its people a joy.
I will rejoice over Jerusalem
>   and take delight in my people;
the sound of weeping and of crying
>   will be heard in it no more.

—ISAIAH 65:17–19

"Now then, at the resurrection, whose wife will she be of the seven, since all of them were married to her?"

Jesus replied, "You are in error because you do not know the Scriptures or the power of God. At the resurrection people will neither marry nor be given in marriage; they will be like the angels in heaven. But about the resurrection of the dead—have you not read what God said to you, 'I am the God of Abraham, the God of Isaac, and the God of Jacob'? He is not the God of the dead but of the living."

—MATTHEW 22:28–32

"For this reason a man will leave his father and mother and be united to his wife, and the two will become one flesh." This is a profound mystery—but I am talking about Christ and the church.

—EPHESIANS 5:31–32

But someone will ask, "How are the dead raised? With what kind of body will they come?" How foolish! What you sow does not come to life unless it dies. When you sow, you do not plant the body that will be, but just a seed, perhaps of wheat or of something else. But God gives it a body as he has determined, and to each kind of seed he gives its own body.

—1 CORINTHIANS 15:35–38

So will it be with the resurrection of the dead. The body that is sown is perishable, it is raised imperishable; it is sown in dishonor, it is raised in glory; it is sown in weakness, it is raised in power; it is sown a natural body, it is raised a spiritual body.

—1 CORINTHIANS 15:42–44

The first man was of the dust of the earth; the second man is of heaven. As was the earthly man, so are those who are of the earth; and as is the heavenly man, so also are those who are of heaven. And just as we have borne the image of the earthly man, so shall we bear the image of the heavenly man.

—1 CORINTHIANS 15:47–49

After this I looked, and there before me was a great multitude that no one could count, from every nation, tribe, people and language, standing before the throne and before the Lamb. They were wearing white robes and were holding palm branches in their hands. And they cried out in a loud voice:

"Salvation belongs to our God,
who sits on the throne,
and to the Lamb."

—REVELATION 7:9–10

Give us this day our daily bread.

—MATTHEW 6:11 ESV

For I tell you I will not drink again from the fruit of the vine until the kingdom of God comes. . . . And I confer on you a kingdom, just as my Father conferred one on me, so that you may eat and drink at my table in my kingdom and sit on thrones, judging the twelve tribes of Israel.

—LUKE 22:18, 29–30

Then the angel said to me, "Write this: Blessed are those who are invited to the wedding supper of the Lamb!" And he added, "These are the true words of God."

—REVELATION 19:9

On this mountain the LORD Almighty will prepare
a feast of rich food for all peoples,
a banquet of aged wine—
the best of meats and the finest of wines.

—ISAIAH 25:6

Everything that lives and moves about will be food for you. Just as I gave you the green plants, I now give you everything.

—GENESIS 9:3

"He will wipe every tear from their eyes. There will be no more death" or mourning or crying or pain, for the old order of things has passed away.

—REVELATION 21:4

For whenever you eat this bread and drink this cup, you proclaim the Lord's death until he comes.

—1 CORINTHIANS 11:26

CHAPTER 6: UNTIL THEN

All these people were still living by faith when they died. They did not receive the things promised; they only saw them and welcomed them from a distance, admitting that they were foreigners and strangers on earth. People who say such things show that they are looking for a country of their own. If they had been thinking of the country they had left, they would have had opportunity to return. Instead, they were longing for a better country—a heavenly one. Therefore God is not ashamed to be called their God, for he has prepared a city for them.

—HEBREWS 11:13–16

But the day of the Lord will come like a thief. The heavens will disappear with a roar; the elements will be destroyed by fire, and the earth and everything done in it will be laid bare.

Since everything will be destroyed in this way, what kind of people ought you to be? You ought to live holy and godly lives as you look forward to the day of God and speed its coming. That day will bring about the destruction of the heavens by fire, and the elements will melt in the heat. But in keeping with his promise we are looking forward to a new heaven and a new earth, where righteousness dwells.

—2 PETER 3:10–13

Their [enemies of the cross] destiny is destruction, their god is their stomach, and their glory is in their shame. Their mind is set on earthly things. But our citizenship is in heaven. And we eagerly await a Savior from there, the Lord Jesus Christ, who, by the power that enables him to bring everything under his control, will transform our lowly bodies so that they will be like his glorious body.

—PHILIPPIANS 3:19–21

And I'll say to myself, "You have plenty of grain laid up for many years. Take life easy; eat, drink and be merry."

—LUKE 12:19

If I fought wild beasts in Ephesus with no more than human hopes, what have I gained? If the dead are not raised,

"Let us eat and drink,
for tomorrow we die."

—1 CORINTHIANS 15:32

But God said to him, "You fool! This very night your life will be demanded from you. Then who will get what you have prepared for yourself?"

—LUKE 12:20

Do not let your hearts be troubled. You believe in God; believe also in me.

—JOHN 14:1

Now faith is confidence in what we hope for and assurance about what we do not see.

—HEBREWS 11:1

By faith Abraham, when called to go to a place he would later receive as his inheritance, obeyed and went, even though he did not know where he was going.

—HEBREWS 11:8

And by faith even Sarah, who was past childbearing age, was enabled to bear children because she considered him faithful who had made the promise.

—HEBREWS 11:11

By faith Abraham, when God tested him, offered Isaac as a sacrifice. He who had embraced the promises was about to sacrifice his one and only son, even though God had said to him, "It is through Isaac that your offspring will be reckoned." Abraham reasoned that God could even raise the dead, and so in a manner of speaking he did receive Isaac back from death.

—HEBREWS 11:17–19

All these people were still living by faith when they died. They did not receive the things promised; they only saw them and welcomed them from a distance, admitting that they were foreigners and strangers on earth. People who say such things show that they are looking for a country of their own. If they had been thinking of the country they had left, they would have had opportunity to return. Instead, they were longing for a better country—a heavenly one. Therefore God is not ashamed to be called their God, for he has prepared a city for them.

—HEBREWS 11:13–16

For he was looking forward to the city with foundations, whose architect and builder is God.

—HEBREWS 11:10

Brothers and sisters, we do not want you to be uninformed about those who sleep in death, so that you do not grieve like the rest of mankind, who have no hope. For we believe that Jesus died and rose again, and so we believe that God will bring with Jesus those who have fallen asleep in him. According to the Lord's word, we tell you that we who are still alive, who are left until the coming of the Lord, will certainly not precede those who have fallen asleep. For the Lord himself will come down from heaven, with a loud command, with the voice of the archangel and with the trumpet call of God, and the dead in Christ will rise first. After that, we who are still alive and are left will be caught up together with them in the clouds to meet the Lord in the air. And so we will be with the Lord forever. Therefore encourage one another with these words.

—1 THESSALONIANS 4:13–18

Therefore we do not lose heart. Though outwardly we are wasting away, yet inwardly we are being renewed day by day. For our light and momentary troubles are achieving for us an eternal glory that far outweighs them all. So we fix our eyes not on what is seen, but on what is unseen, since what is seen is temporary, but what is unseen is eternal.

—2 CORINTHIANS 4:16–18

But you will receive power when the Holy Spirit comes on you; and you will be my witnesses in Jerusalem, and in all Judea and Samaria, and to the ends of the earth.

—ACTS 1:8

He who testifies to these things says, "Yes, I am coming soon." Amen. Come, Lord Jesus.

—REVELATION 22:20

Q&A ON LIFE NOW

See that you do not despise one of these little ones. For I tell you that their angels in heaven always see the face of my Father in heaven.

—MATTHEW 18:10

Are not all angels ministering spirits sent to serve those who will inherit salvation?

—HEBREWS 1:14

In a loud voice they were saying:

> "Worthy is the Lamb, who was slain,
> to receive power and wealth and wisdom and strength
> and honor and glory and praise!"
>
> —REVELATION 5:12

Then I looked and heard the voice of many angels, numbering thousands upon thousands, and ten thousand times ten thousand. They encircled the throne and the living creatures and the elders.

> —REVELATION 5:11

Do you think I cannot call on my Father, and he will at once put at my disposal more than twelve legions of angels?

> —MATTHEW 26:53

Then Jesus was led by the Spirit into the wilderness to be tempted by the devil. After fasting forty days and forty nights, he was hungry. The tempter came to him and said, "If you are the Son of God, tell these stones to become bread."

Jesus answered, "It is written: 'Man shall not live on bread alone, but on every word that comes from the mouth of God.'"

Then the devil took him to the holy city and had him stand on the highest point of the temple. "If you are the Son of God," he said, "throw yourself down. For it is written:

> "'He will command his angels concerning you,
> and they will lift you up in their hands,
> so that you will not strike your foot against a stone.'"

Jesus answered him, "It is also written: 'Do not put the Lord your God to the test.'"

Again, the devil took him to a very high mountain and showed him all the kingdoms of the world and their splendor. "All this I will give you," he said, "if you will bow down and worship me."

Jesus said to him, "Away from me, Satan! For it is written: 'Worship the Lord your God, and serve him only.'"

Then the devil left him, and angels came and attended him.

—MATTHEW 4:1–11

An angel from heaven appeared to him and strengthened him.

—LUKE 22:43

My God sent his angel, and he shut the mouths of the lions. They have not hurt me, because I was found innocent in his sight. Nor have I ever done any wrong before you, Your Majesty.

—DANIEL 6:22

Be alert and of sober mind. Your enemy the devil prowls around like a roaring lion looking for someone to devour. Resist him, standing firm in the faith, because you know that the family of believers throughout the world is undergoing the same kind of sufferings.

—1 PETER 5:8–9

For our struggle is not against flesh and blood, but against the rulers, against the authorities, against the powers of this dark world and against the spiritual forces of evil in the heavenly realms.

—EPHESIANS 6:12

For he will command his angels concerning you to guard you in all your ways.

—PSALM 91:11

The time came when the beggar died and the angels carried him to Abraham's side.

—LUKE 16:22

By the sweat of your brow
      you will eat your food
until you return to the ground,
      since from it you were taken;
for dust you are
      and to dust you will return.

—GENESIS 3:19

This is what the LORD says:

"For three sins of Moab,
      even for four, I will not relent.
Because he burned to ashes
      the bones of Edom's king."

—AMOS 2:1

He who testifies to these things says, "Yes, I am coming soon."
      Amen. Come, Lord Jesus.

—REVELATION 22:20

But about that day or hour no one knows, not even the angels in heaven, nor the Son, but only the Father.

—MATTHEW 24:36

But do not forget this one thing, dear friends: With the Lord a day is like a thousand years, and a thousand years are like a day. The Lord is not slow in keeping his promise, as some understand slowness. Instead he is patient with you, not wanting anyone to perish, but everyone to come to repentance.

—2 PETER 3:8–9

And this gospel of the kingdom will be preached in the whole world as a testimony to all nations, and then the end will come.

—MATTHEW 24:14

So they took away the stone. Then Jesus looked up and said, "Father, I thank you that you have heard me. I knew that you always hear me, but I said this for the benefit of the people standing here, that they may believe that you sent me."

—JOHN 11:41–42

But Stephen, full of the Holy Spirit, looked up to heaven and saw the glory of God, and Jesus standing at the right hand of God. "Look," he said, "I see heaven open and the Son of Man standing at the right hand of God."

—ACTS 7:55–56

I know a man in Christ who fourteen years ago was caught up to the third heaven. Whether it was in the body or out of the body I do not know—God knows. And I know that this man—whether in the body or apart from the body I do not know, but God knows—was caught up to paradise and heard inexpressible things, things that no one is permitted to tell.

—2 CORINTHIANS 12:2–4

He who descended is the very one who ascended higher than all the heavens, in order to fill the whole universe.

—EPHESIANS 4:10

Abraham replied, "They have Moses and the Prophets; let them listen to them." . . . He said to him, "If they do not listen to Moses and the Prophets, they will not be convinced even if someone rises from the dead."

—LUKE 16:29, 31

Notes

Introduction

1. Roger E. Olson, *The Mosaic of Christian Belief: Twenty Centuries of Unity and Diversity* (Downers Grove, IL: IVP, 2002), 330.

Chapter 1: Is Jesus Enough?

1. Gennie Coe, "Jesus IS Life," *Journey to the Hills* (blog), June 16, 2016, https://journeytothehills.com//?s=Jesus+is+enough&search=Go.

Chapter 2: What Happens If I Die Without Christ?

1. "Death Cafe Worldwide Map," Death Café, accessed August 31, 2016, http://deathcafe.com/map/.
2. Larry Copeland, "Life Expectancy in the USA Hits a Record High," *USA Today*, October 8, 2014, http://www.usatoday.com /story/news/nation/2014/10/08/us-life-expectancy-hits-record-high /16874039/.
3. Walter A. Elwell, ed., *Evangelical Dictionary of Theology* (Grand Rapids: Baker, 1984), 492.
4. C. S. Lewis, *The Problem of Pain*, rev. ed. (New York: HarperOne, 2015), 130.

Chapter 3: What Happens If I Die with Christ?

1. Woody Allen quoted in Joanne Laucius, "Death Wishes: What We Want Versus What We Get," *Ottawa Citizen*, February 10, 2015,

http://ottawacitizen.com/news/local-news/death-wishes-what-we-want -versus-what-we-get.

2. From my study of the use of the word *paradise*, it seems most consistent to say it is the residence, or "abode," of the righteous. The garden of Eden in Genesis 2:8–10 was Paradise, or a place of bliss, for Adam and Eve. In Luke 23:43 Jesus refers to paradise as the abode of the righteous dead or a portion of Hades for the righteous dead. This was consistent with Jewish beliefs (*The Zondervan Pictorial Encyclopedia of the Bible*, rev. ed., s.v. "paradise"). At the resurrection of Jesus, paradise, or the abode of the righteous dead, was moved to be where the presence of God is, in heaven. At the return of Jesus for the establishment of the new earth, the Edenic garden in the center of the city of Jerusalem—where the Tree of Life resides—is called "the paradise of God" (Revelation 2:7).

3. Kenny Chesney, "Everybody Wants to Go to Heaven" (with the Wailers) in *Lucky Old Sun*, Blue Chair Records and BMG Music, 2008.

4. The National Institute of Mental Health. "Fear/Phobia Statistics," Statistic Brain, research conducted April 27, 2015, http://www .statisticbrain.com/fear-phobia-statistics/.

Q&A on Life In Between

1. *The Merriam-Webster Dictionary*, new edition, s.v. "ghost."

2. J. Carl Laney, "Ghost, Demon, or Hallucination: Did Samuel Return from the Dead?" *Transformed* blog, Western Seminary, June 27, 2014, https://www.westernseminary.edu/transformedblog/2014/06/27/ghost -demon-or-hallucination-did-samuel-return-from-the-dead/.

3. Popular Jewish superstition held that the appearance of spirits during the night brought disaster. The disciples' terror was prompted by what they may have thought was a water spirit. *NIV Study Bible* (Grand Rapids: Zondervan, 2011), 1667.

4. http://www.kingjamesbibleonline.org/Apocrypha-Books/ and http://www.bible-researcher.com/canon2.html.

5. Walter A. Elwell, ed., *Evangelical Dictionary of Theology* (Grand Rapids: Baker, 1984), 897.

6. Film clips at "Clarence, Angel Second Class, From 'It's a Wonderful Life,'" YouTube video, 1:54, posted by Clarence Cromwell, January 19, 2014, https://www.youtube.com/watch?v=v2ZZUu2HUuo.

Chapter 4: What Happens If I Don't Know Christ When He Returns?

1. John Grisham, *The Innocent Man* (New York: Doubleday, 2006); Jim Dwyer, "Ronald Williamson, Freed from Death Row, Dies at 51," *New York Times*, December 9, 2004, http://www.nytimes.com /2004/12/09/us/ronald-williamson-freed-from-death-row-dies-at -51.html.

2. For further information, see video by Glenn Peoples on *Rethinking Hell*, http://www.rethinkinghell.com/2012/11/deprived-of-continuance -irenaeus-the-conditionalist/.

3. "Church Fathers Who Were Conditionalists," https://www.youtube .com/watch?v=je3AW6QeXzk.

4. Peoples, *Rethinking Hell*.

5. Conditional immortality: the belief that eternal life or immortality is conditioned on the acceptance of Christ's offer for the forgiveness of sins.

6. Roger E. Olson, *The Mosaic of Christian Belief: Twenty Centuries of Unity and Diversity* (Downer's Grove, IL: IVP, 2002), 321, 328.

Chapter 5: What Happens If I Do Know Christ When He Returns?

1. Olson, *The Mosaic of Christian Belief*, 314.

2. The National Institute of Mental Health. "Fear/Phobia Statistics," Statistic Brain, research conducted April 27, 2015, http://www .statisticbrain.com/fear-phobia-statistics/.

3. "The Jetsons (theme song)," YouTube video, 58, season 3 theme song, posted by Warner Archive, December 19, 2014, https://www .youtube.com/watch?v=tTq6Tofmo7E.

4. Ron Rhodes, *The Wonder of Heaven* (Eugene, OR: Harvest House, 2009), 122.

5. D. A. Carson, *The Gospel According to John* (Grand Rapids: Eerdmans, 1991), 489.

Q&A on Life Forever

1. Thomas Aquinas, *Summa Theologica*, supplement, q. 81, art. 1.

Chapter 6: Until Then

1. J. I. Packer, *Never Beyond Hope: How God Touches and Uses Imperfect People* (Downers Grove, IL: IVP, 2005).

2. Randy Frazee, *The Christian Life Profile Assessment Tool Workbook: Discovering the Quality of Your Relationships* (Grand Rapids: Zondervan, 2005).

3. Negrospirituals.com, accessed September 7, 2016, http://www .negrospirituals.com/index.html.

About the Author

RANDY FRAZEE COMMITTED HIS LIFE TO BEING A pastor at the age of fifteen, the same year he met his wife, Rozanne. He has served in three churches over the last thirty years. He currently serves as senior minister at the Oak Hills Church in San Antonio, Texas. Randy is the architect of the exciting The Story church engagement campaign and general editor of the Believe engagement campaign. He is also the author of *The Heart of the Story*; *Think, Act, Be Like Jesus*; *The Connecting Church 2.0*; and *The Christian Life Profile Assessment Tool*. Randy adores his four grown children, their spouses, and his two grandkids. He plays the banjo, is hooked on golf, and savors times around the table with family and neighbors. Rozanne, his wife, is his BFF.